D0429073

WILLIE

THE GAME-CHANGING STORY OF THE NHL'S FIRST BLACK PLAYER

WILLIE O'REE

WITH MICHAEL McKINLEY

VIKING

VIKING

an imprint of Penguin Canada, a division of Penguin Random House Canada Limited

Canada • USA • UK • Ireland • Australia • New Zealand • India • South Africa • China

First published 2020

www.penguinrandomhouse.ca

LIBRARY AND ARCHIVES CANADA CATALOGUING IN PUBLICATION
Title: Willie : the game-changing story of the NHL's first black player / Willie O'Ree
    with Michael McKinley
Names: O'Ree, Willie, 1935- author. | McKinley, Michael, 1961- author.
Identifiers: Canadiana (print) 20200179535 | Canadiana (ebook) 20200179543 |
    ISBN 9780735239746 (hardcover) | ISBN 9780735239753 (HTML)
Subjects: LCSH: O'Ree, Willie, 1935- | LCSH: Hockey players—Canada—Biography. |
    CSH: Black Canadian hockey players—Biography | LCGFT: Autobiographies.
Classification: LCC GV848.5.O69 A3 2020 | DDC 796.962092—dc23

All photos are from Willie O'Ree's personal collection unless otherwise specified.
Book design by Andrew Roberts
Cover design: Andrew Roberts
Cover image: Portrait of Willie O'Ree by Tim Okamura, originally commissioned for the acclaimed documentary *Willie*, produced and directed by Laurence Mathieu-Leger, Bryant McBride, and Ebyan Bihi. Williedoc.com

Printed and bound in the United States of America

10 9 8 7 6 5 4 3 2 1

Penguin
Random House
VIKING CANADA

To everyone who had a dream
and was told "no, you can't," but
found a way to find the "yes, I can."

CONTENTS

FOREWORD

In many ways, I grew up like Willie O'Ree: in a small Canadian town, playing every sport available, especially baseball and hockey.

Also, I was often the only minority kid on the team.

Not that it usually made much difference. My friends never made me conscious of this fact. My teammates didn't seem to notice. Why should I care?

Well, for one thing, the world isn't made up just of friends and teammates. It would be a lot easier if it were.

I clearly remember the first time someone pointed out to me that my color was different from the other kids playing hockey. I was at a tournament just outside of Edmonton, the first tournament I'd ever been to. I was playing Novice "C" (or Shaver "C", as it was called back then). I could barely skate.

I had just played, and I was standing in line at the concession booth, waiting to get some fries. There were a couple of kids from another team ahead of me. For some reason, one of them turned around. Our eyes met briefly, then he did a double-take. Then he asked a question Willie O'Ree must have been asked a lot more often than I was.

"Why are *you* playing hockey? Black people don't play hockey."

Who knows what was going through that kid's mind at the time. I remember his face clearly to this day, and I remember just as unmistakably the expression on it, and the tone of his voice, both of which told me that his intentions were not friendly, or curious. He was suggesting that I didn't belong in hockey.

One of the reasons I remember that tournament so vividly is that I didn't have an answer for that kid. I was stung. Of course I was. I was just seven years old. That kind of unfriendliness just doesn't make sense to a seven-year-old. So I wasn't just hurt; I was confused.

Naturally, I told my mom. She said not to worry about what other kids say. She said black people are amazing athletes and amazing people. She said I could play or be whatever I wanted. And she had proof. She just told me to look at Grant Fuhr. My mother wasn't a big hockey buff, but there was no one in Alberta who didn't know who Grant Fuhr was. She was right, of course. Black people do play hockey. I also remember my dad telling me not to see color but to see people as individuals— that I am no better or less than anyone else because of my skin color. I was very fortunate as well that I had my grandparents, who were very helpful with words of encouragement. My grandmother in particular always knew just what I needed to hear.

After those conversations, I knew what to say the next time someone told me I didn't belong.

That is to say, I came to understand something Willie talks about in his book. Racism never stopped me from being a hockey player. Not even close. Sure, there have been ignorant or rude people over the years. But you know what? Those people who tried to pass on their own issues to others almost always brought out the best in the people around me.

When I was playing minor hockey, a parent from the other team might shout something meant to discourage me.

It happened. Not often, but it happened. And invariably, a parent from our team would go over and have a word. That means the world to a kid. My mom and my grandpa came to most of my games, but it wouldn't have been the same if they had felt they had to stand up for me, so it was comforting that there were other parents who stepped up, and helped to make me more confident that I belonged in the game, and that it was the person in the stands who didn't belong.

And sure, I heard that kind of language on the ice from time to time, but my teammates have always had my back. Willie says the same thing happened when he played. Hockey is like that. On any good team, the things that make you different don't matter. It's the things you have in common that pull you together. When you're wearing the same sweater, nothing else should matter.

So no, racism never stopped me from being a hockey player. But it did stop me from being *just* a hockey player. Whether I wanted it or not, I was always a black hockey player.

Not that I minded being a black hockey player. But it was a reminder of how difficult the road ahead could have been for me. If you're a white kid, you probably never have to think about these things, because every one of your heroes looks like you. Everyone in the Hockey Hall of Fame looks like you. The guy hoisting the Stanley Cup looks like you. Every number one draft pick looks like you. In fact, everyone in the whole draft. You get the picture.

That's no one's fault. But it does make it hard to dream about the NHL as a career when you're black. Harder, anyway. But I definitely had those dreams. So naturally, I was always aware of the careers of black players in the NHL. It is impossible to exaggerate what Claude Vilgrain meant to me as a kid. Or Tony McKegney. You're never going to accomplish something you don't dream of, and I know that seeing stars like Fuhr made my dream feasible.

Don't get me wrong. I had a lot of the same idols as the other kids. I loved Gretzky and wanted to be like Messier, but it was people like Fuhr, Vilgrain, and McKegney who kept my dream alive. They gave me an answer for whenever the same awkward question came up.

I wish I had known about Willie O'Ree back then. Maybe McKegney and Vilgrain knew about him, but I didn't. I wasn't much of a history buff—I was just a kid in love with sports, hockey, and the Oilers, in that order. Later on, I learned about his legacy, of course. It would have been impossible not to. But I didn't meet Willie until my rookie year in the NHL.

I broke into the league in 1996–97. As it happens, Willie came *back* into the league, with the NHL's diversity program, just the year before. I was at an event in Raleigh, North Carolina, put on by the league to make sure minority kids knew that they were welcome in our game. We were playing road hockey with kids who barely knew which end of the stick to hold, but everyone was having a blast. Then a member of the NHL head office brought over an older gentleman to introduce him. That's when I met the Jackie Robinson of hockey.

It's hard to explain the effect of meeting Willie O'Ree. I don't just mean as a black hockey player. He is as warm and good-natured as anyone you'll ever meet. He's not looking for attention, not looking for the spotlight. If you talk to Willie for five minutes, it will be clear that he's there just because he wants to help. Shake his hand, and you'll realize that he could probably have crushed a billiard ball back when he was in his prime. Willie must have been a handful when he played.

How good was Willie O'Ree? For one thing, he played back when there were only six teams in the league. So that tells you that he was one of the best 132 players in the world back then. Today, a spot on an NHL roster means you're one of the best 713. So Willie was *good*.

But there is more. As you may already know, Willie played with only one eye. I couldn't believe that when I heard it. And he suffered the injury *before* he made the NHL. He could easily have called it a career after a severe injury like that. I can't even imagine playing the game without peripheral vision, and without depth perception. To break into the best league in the world, and to put up the kind of numbers Willie did over the course of his professional career, while working against that kind of disadvantage, is nothing short of astonishing.

Hockey can get a little dirty at times. If a hockey player thinks he can get away with something, he'll try. If he thinks he can intimidate you, he will. And it works. Some guys don't want to fight through that every shift. And when you watch highlights of old games, you see that guys got away with a lot more back then. It's not easy being a hockey player, and it was even harder back when Willie played.

But Willie wasn't just a hockey player. He was a black hockey player. He was the only black hockey player, the first. He knew that every eye was on him, every shift. I can only imagine the target a black rookie would have had on his back in 1958. He knew that every pest and every tough guy and every loudmouth fan thought they could get under his skin. And I'm sure they tried. He would be navigating the ice with his one good eye, not knowing where the attack might come from, but knowing that, in some ways, he was all alone, because he was the first. And Willie just put on that smile, and went out there, and showed them how it's done.

That is *tough*.

As Willie says in these pages, there were great black players before him, who never got their chance. It's impossible to know exactly why. But I wonder if coaches and GMs recognized in Willie not only the skill to make it in the world's best league, but also the discipline and attitude it would take to be a pioneer in that league, knowing it would be an uphill battle. Not everyone can skate uphill. Willie can. Willie did.

One thing you'll never hear from Willie O'Ree is a complaint. He never had it easy, but I get the impression that he always knew he was blessed, too. He got to fulfill a childhood dream. And he got the chance to live a life that helps others. That is a blessing.

But there is one blessing every black hockey player has had since 1958 that Willie did not. We all had footsteps to follow in. But Willie never did. Willie O'Ree is the only one who made it without anyone showing him the way. I know what a trailblazer like Willie means to those kids, because I was that kid.

And now I know that when someone asks, "Why do *you* play hockey?" Willie O'Ree has answered the question already.

Jarome Iginla, *June 2020*

1.

THE FIRST BEGINNING

Every story has a beginning, a middle, and an end, something we were taught back in elementary school in Fredericton, New Brunswick, where I was born. It's a lesson that has stayed with me for more than eighty years—although, in my life's journey, I feel that I'm far closer to the middle than to the end. As for the beginning, I might politely disagree with my teachers. I've had more than one beginning in my long life. You could say I've had as many as there are chapters in this book. You could also say that I'm not yet done with beginnings. In fact, I am counting on them.

But let me start in the autumn of 1935, when the maple leaves in Fredericton have turned their brightest shade of red and when I came into the world. Fredericton is a small city today, with nearly sixty thousand people calling it home, but it was tiny when I began in this world on the fifteenth of October, the thirteenth child—although only nine of us survived birth—of Harry and Rosebud O'Ree.

I come from a long line of Canadians, stretching back to the late eighteenth century. That's when my ancestor Paris O'Ree made his way here from the United States—and we think he came on an early version of the Underground Railroad, that network of trails and safe houses set up to help fleeing slaves escape to Canada. Paris had been "owned" by Lieutenant-Colonel Peter Horry, an officer in South Carolina who fought against the British during the American War of Independence, from 1775 to 1783.

I've been lucky enough to research archives in South Carolina to find out more about how my family became connected to his. His surname, Horry, looks as though it's pronounced "hoary," but instead it's pronounced "o-ree," in keeping with his family's French Huguenot background. So no, I don't come from a long line of Irishmen. The reality is much darker. As part of their payment for services in the army, officers of the South Carolina regiments received "three grown negroes and one small negro" to be their slaves. And so, as Peter Horry's slave, Paris took on his name.

We can only surmise that Paris O'Ree, as the name came to be spelled, reached Canada sometime in the late 1700s, since his son Henry was born in 1791 in Kings County, New Brunswick. We don't know exactly how Paris won his freedom, but I sure wish we did. There's probably a story there that would make the generations of O'Rees that followed him proud. All we know is that somehow our ancestor's courage, his willingness to act according to what's right, is what our family grew from. And it's something from which we all take inspiration.

Kings County was, and still is, a community of small towns and farms that calls itself the dairy capital of New Brunswick. The area is also known for its sixteen covered bridges. (Or, as we called them, kissing bridges—a term dating back to the days when a boy would stop his horse-drawn buggy halfway across so that he and his girl could have some privacy.) It was in the rich soil of this area that Paris O'Ree seems to have made a go of it as a farmer, since land deeds show that he bought just over two hundred acres here, which he sold in 1810.

Henry's son William was born around 1837, and then *his* son Charles was born around 1867. And in Fredericton in June 1891, William's son Henry, my father, who went by "Harry," was born. My mother, Rosebud, was born there three years later. Then, on September 24, 1913, my parents were married. My father was twenty-one and my mother just nineteen.

So I am the great-great-grandson of a man who was enslaved, a man whose dreams of a better future propelled him to start a new life in another new world. I can see him in my mind's eye, this man who was stolen from his homeland, given a new name and as payment to another man. I can imagine Paris O'Ree spotting his chance and taking it. I am proud of him. For without his taking that risk, putting his life on the line to find freedom, I wouldn't be here now. And there's more than a little bit of him in me.

In any case, I'd say that counts as a beginning. None of what follows would have come about without Paris O'Ree.

Three years after my parents were married, their nine very active children started appearing—first my eldest sister, Violet, in 1916, followed by my eldest brother, Richard, in 1918. Seventeen years and six surviving kids later, I came along as the last in the line.

Let me elaborate a bit here: my mother gave birth to two sets of twins who died—one set in childbirth, the other shortly after they were born. I can't imagine the pain and sorrow this must have caused my parents. But they bore it, as they bore everything, with dignity and grace.

And they had nine other children to think about. By today's standards we had a huge family, but in those days families had to be huge—not all children survived, as we knew too well, and there was no government safety net to look after people in their old age. Social Security was established in the United States in 1935—the year I was born, in the middle of the Great Depression—but social insurance wouldn't come to Canada until almost thirty years later, in 1964. (By the way, that was the same year the country got the red and white flag with the maple leaf on it. Until then we'd gazed upon the Red Ensign, a British naval flag, in the hockey rinks I played in until I was nearly thirty years old.)

Violet was nineteen and Richard seventeen when I was born, so they were almost like an aunt and uncle to me when I was growing up. The rest of us were jammed in between:

Thelma, Alfred, Margaret, Lewis, Robert, and Betty, who was two years older than I. And then the baby, which was me.

We lived in a rented two-story, maroon-shingled house at 212 Charlotte Street. When you walked in you'd enter the living room, and then straight on from there was the dining room, kitchen, and utility room. The bedrooms and bathroom were upstairs. Across the road lived the Lawrences, who were the other black family in Fredericton. Mrs. Lawrence just adored my mother, who would bake her cakes and pies and I suppose was a kind of daughter to her, but it was a friendship based on affection, not on color. Meanwhile, my grandparents from both parents' sides lived in Gagetown, a small community outside of Fredericton where a lot of black families lived. (Two other places that were home mainly to black people were Spring Hill, where we had friends, and Barker's Point, outside of town on the Saint John River, where Richard lived once he'd moved out of the house.) We were close to our grandparents growing up; we'd go up to see them and play cards or they'd come down to see us.

My father, Harry, was smart—he loved to read the papers—and hardworking, too. For nearly forty years he worked in Fredericton's road maintenance industry, cleaning the streets of debris and snow and eventually rising to crew supervisor. Then, after he retired, he acted as a patrol guard for the schools, making sure kids could cross the street safely. Harry was a relatively small man, about 135 pounds soaking wet, but he was strong and wiry. He was also an excellent baseball player, his pitch sure and hard. And, as I can imagine now, he was a man consumed with providing for his wife and children, which he did with fortitude and discipline.

Harry was a complete gentleman, who always wore a fedora. When he passed by a woman on the street, he would tip his hat and bid the lady good day. I wear a fedora now as well, and do the same. My father's courtesy has stuck with me.

So has his competitive spirit. He was ferocious in contest—you didn't want to play the wrong card if you were on his team playing Forty-Fives, a Maritime card game that I love, one not unlike Euchre. I would see him leave the table in disgust when a partner played a wrong card. My friends say that I sometimes do the same, but I believe they exaggerate. I just like to win, and aim to win all the time. So if I rise from the table during a game, I might just be standing up for a stretch.

Rosebud, on the other hand, didn't care what card you played. She was a loving, caring, tireless mother to us all, with a big, ready smile for everyone. But she did care about her appearance and would dress to the nines every time she stepped out of our house. I like to dress well when I'm in public, and I get that from her. So both my parents are still very much with me, even though they've long since passed on.

By the time I was ten most of my brothers and sisters had moved away. There was just Betty and me living at home. My other sisters were all married, Richard was married, Robert and Lewis were living away from home, and Alfred had passed away in 1949. So there was no big crush to get into the bathroom in the morning. In any case, that was never an issue for me—thanks to hockey, I've always been an early riser. And

I like to be early, so if I set my alarm for five thirty a.m., I'll be up and running by five fifteen. Once I'm awake, I stay that way until my afternoon nap, the cherished ritual of pro hockey players everywhere.

But even though I was the youngest, my mother made sure I didn't take advantage of her. If she said be home at ten o'clock, I was home at ten o'clock, not a minute later. If I didn't show up on time I'd be grounded and have to stay in on weekends. So I accepted the house rules and usually kept to them.

Not always, though. When John "Junior" Doherty, my great friend then and now, would come by with a ladder, I'd climb down from my second-floor bedroom and off we'd go to the movies. (Then, when I'd come home late, I'd climb back up.) This was during the Second World War, and while it was a terrible time for the world, it was a wonderful time for movies, among them such gems as *Casablanca* and *Pride of the Yankees*. I especially loved westerns, like *Buffalo Bill* and *The Yellow Rose of Texas*. I did get caught a couple of times by Rosebud O'Ree, house arrest being the result. But she never held a grudge. Neither did I. I knew the game.

My sister Betty, who was a couple of years older, got away with much more than I did. Or maybe it just seemed that way. She would climb out her bedroom window too sometimes, and I don't know when she came home because I didn't stay awake to find out. I kept her secret, though, just as one day she would keep mine.

Life in Fredericton was good. When I was growing up, it was a little place, with a population of just ten thousand in the year I was born. And even though the city's two black families, the O'Rees and the Lawrences, lived on the same street—an easy walk to downtown and to the Saint John River—that was based on coincidence, and again not on color.

Nor was my childhood defined by race, as my friends and I didn't judge each other by what shade of the rainbow we happened to be. This is not to say that Canada didn't have problems, as it certainly did (and does) when it comes to its history with the Indigenous population. And to be sure, people of color have experienced prejudice and bigotry, as have people whose first language is French, or just not English. (When I was a kid in Fredericton, though, English was the language everyone spoke. I did take French in school, but the city and province didn't become bilingual until much later.) There will always be good people, just as there will always be those who view the dissimilarity of others as a threat. Fredericton was no different in that regard. We had our fair allocation of human nature.

But my childhood was free of anyone bullying me because of my color. Along with my friend Mike Coster, I loved being part of the local Cub Scouts and Boy Scouts, whose meetings were held at St. Anne's, an Anglican church I went to with my mother and sister and where Mike's dad was the minister. We'd go on an annual trip to a campsite about fifty miles north of the city, where I learned how to survive in the wilderness—how to build a lean-to, start a fire, and avoid getting eaten by bears. I looked forward to making that amazing trip every year until I was about fourteen.

My best pals also included Gus Mazzuca, who is Italian, and Louis George, who is Lebanese, and of course Junior Doherty, who is Irish, but we were all just Canadian kids growing up at a time when the world was fighting a terrible war. Looking back, the funny thing is that the war is remembered for having settled the question of whether different ethnic groups should live alongside each other. And there we were, a bunch of pals, settling the question every day, with a side business in standard childhood mischief.

Though war is unquestionably a terrible thing, and there was always a sense in the air that everyone was eager for it to end, those who lived through it tend to remember it as a time when everything seemed to matter more somehow. Friends and family. Right and wrong. People may not have been happier in the usual sense, but the way they remember it, they were more *alive*, perhaps because so much was at stake.

In any case, mine was a very happy childhood. I was loved, looked after, and allowed to play any game I wanted with anyone I wanted to play that game with.

And my first game was hockey—the game that would go on to make me who I am. Hockey has given me a great life. But when I took my first steps on the ice more than eighty years ago, all I knew was that this was a much better way to get around than walking. And that I never wanted to stop. This game on ice was the beginning of me.

2.

THE SECOND BEGINNING

I started skating a bit before the Second World War began, when I was just three years old. My father would unroll the garden hose, spray water on the frozen back lawn, and just like that, we had a rink. The first freeze came in November and the thaw began in mid-March, so the outdoor skating season was a long one. The frozen ponds, creeks, and rivers of Fredericton were to become my ice rinks, but I started in our backyard.

Since I was so young, I began my life on the ice with a primitive type of beginner's skates, which were common at the time: two blocks of wood with two metal blades on the bottom of each, like training wheels on a bike. Attached to each block were two leather straps that my father would loop over my shoes and then tighten up. Then he'd send me out on the ice.

My father, who didn't skate, and my eldest brother, Richard, who did, watched over me, but I pretty much taught myself by pushing an old chair in front of me for balance, as generations of Canadians have done. That's how we still do it, and how I help kids learn to skate today.

When I graduated to skating without the chair, if I fell down, I would just get back up and go again. It's much easier to fall when you're little, and it can even seem fun (although as a player I was always strong on my skates; it would take a lot to knock me off stride, let alone to the ice). Once I was able to glide, my father gave me a hockey stick—and I learned that this was much better for balance than any chair. And then, when I felt the weight of the puck on the end of that stick, I knew that if I could skate, I could play hockey.

When you're three years old you haven't really been walking all that long, but I remember that skating felt like the best thing ever—if we didn't have wings, well, we could fly on skates. I loved it from the start. And my goal was to be the best skater in the province.

I played a lot of pond hockey. We tend to romanticize pond hockey, but once you play on a manufactured rink (indoors or out), you realize how rough the ice of a pond can be. That's because the wind whips the water and it freezes unevenly, with craters and little ice hills all over the pond. Kids today may have a hard time imagining the game on ponds and rivers. Bubbles form in the ice and crack under the pressure of skate blades, creating little hazards. Twigs and leaves freeze into the ice, and because they absorb sunlight faster than the ice around them, they heat up and create little soft spots where skate blades will stick. Natural ice also chips more easily than indoor ice, meaning the rink quickly gets so rutted that your skates chatter and the puck skips around erratically.

It makes skating bumpy, but it does wonders for your stick-handling. If you can control the puck on the blade of your stick while you're bouncing around the pond, you can sure control it in the arena. And you need to keep your head up! So I'm glad I learned the game on the pond and sorry to see that tradition disappearing. On the other hand, I'm happy that kids have good rinks where they can learn to skate and play the great game on ice.

New Brunswick is Canada's third smallest province, but it's still pretty large, covering an area that's a bit bigger than New Jersey, Massachusetts, Connecticut, and Maryland combined. So I had a lot of room to skate. And by the time I was five I was skating every day during the winter, even when it was snowing. We'd take a shovel, clear the snow, and off we'd go. If it snowed we'd take a break, clear the rink, and then skate some more. It had to be pretty harsh weather to keep me off the ice. (A blizzard might have been enough to make me think about giving it a miss.) One of my favorite things to do was skate to school, right along the roads and sidewalks of the city. Then, as soon as I'd arrive, I'd pretty much time my day by the minutes ticking down until I could put my skates back on and skate home. Side streets weren't plowed back then, so passing cars would pack the snow down into ice, turning Fredericton into a giant, mazelike skating rink.

I've mentioned that my brother Richard (we called him Coot, the nickname his hockey team gave him because I guess he reminded them of the bird) was seventeen years older than me. He was a hockey player and a boxer of talent, and would go on to become the amateur light-heavyweight champion of the Maritimes (New Brunswick, Nova Scotia, and Prince Edward Island). He was also my mentor, and a very good teacher. Since my dad didn't skate it was Coot who taught me hockey, gently at first—we'd practice passing and shooting—and then, as I grew up, challenging me more. He knew I had athletic talent but wouldn't let me off the hook when it came to working hard at a game. He made me do skating drills: crossover turning left, crossover turning right, stopping left, stopping right, backwards skating. When you're little and just learning how to play, these are the skills you need to master, repeating them again and again until you take them for granted and can do them without thinking.

Most kids want to do the minimum. They want to be able to skate just well enough to chase the puck. But Coot knew that skating is the foundation of everything; every other skill builds on it. And in today's NHL, that's truer than ever. Coot was a little ahead of his time.

Coot was patient, though, and was kind to me. It was as if he knew I'd go further in hockey than he would, and so he wanted to give me every chance at achieving hockey's highest rung—the NHL. Though I wasn't thinking NHL yet. I was thinking about playing on a team and having my own jersey.

And so I did, when at the age of five I started playing in an organized league at Wilmot Park, less than a ten-minute walk from my home in Fredericton's west end. (And my first jersey was orange and black, like a tiger, which pleased me greatly.) When I started playing organized hockey, we didn't even have benches—just an outdoor rink with boards around it. Sometimes the snow would be piled up so high around them that people would just stand on the banks, looking down at us during our games. I didn't actually play in my first indoor rink until I was fifteen.

We didn't have any blue lines painted on the ice, nor did we have any faceoff circles. We just had a red dot painted where the puck should be dropped. But the game was still evolving, as games do. Hockey had been using the blue line only since 1918, and the red line wasn't introduced until 1943, if you can believe it. When a game stops changing, its time might be up.

One of the least fun parts of outdoor hockey was dealing with mid-game snowstorms. We'd have to stop and sweep the snow off the rink, but if Mother Nature was in a mood, the snow would sometimes fall faster than we could sweep. The puck would start to slow down and we'd have to call the game off. That really annoyed me, since you'd be either in the middle of winning or in the middle of a glorious comeback.

I was a left-handed shot and played left wing throughout my early career. The names of the age groups are changing in Canada, but back then we used the old names. First I played novice, then atom, then pee-wee. Then I played bantam, midget, junior. Funny how a kid who plays bantam looks like a giant to a novice.

I was always ready to play hockey when I was a kid, and my routine didn't change too much. We usually had Saturday morning games, so I'd eat a little breakfast—toast and jam and maybe some fruit because I didn't want to be too weighed down. I'd put on all my gear at home, except for my skates. After all, we didn't have locker rooms at the outdoor rink. We didn't even have sheds where you could warm yourself up between periods.

My gear was pretty simple. I wore shin guards, a protective cup, hockey pants, elbow pads, shoulder pads, and gloves. Hockey equipment today is lighter and tougher, and since it fits the contours of your body much more closely, it gives more protection. I still have my equipment from the last year I played pro, but compared to the gear of today, it's as if we were dressed for a costume party.

Before I'd get out onto the rink, my parents would be there on the sidelines, telling me to be careful; they didn't want me to get hurt. I'd always be ready, though, and would do a warm-up on the ice—skating fast, stopping hard, shooting on goal, kind of imagining how I wanted to play the game I was about to play. But not in any sports psychologist sort of way. I was just a kid who loved the game and was now scoring the winning goal in my head before the puck was even dropped—and I couldn't wait for that puck to get dropped.

My parents weren't as lucky as they waited for the game to start, having to bounce up and down to keep warm and then to keep bouncing as they watched me play. They used to come to all my games, even when I was a little guy. It's good to have someone cheering you on, and I used to play extra hard for them—I knew they'd believed in me from the very beginning of my life as an athlete.

There was no hanging around talking about the game afterward, either: it was too cold. We'd all just pile into our parents' cars and head for home. I'd have a shower, wash my underwear, hang up my shoulder pads. Then I'd wait for the next game.

Hockey thrilled me. It was a kind of life force for me. I had to keep skating, and I had to play hockey, and if I did those things, I felt like I could do anything. I loved the feel of the wind rushing by as I flew along the ice. I loved the sound of ice chips spraying when I hit the brakes and spun around to charge back the other way. I loved feeling the puck hit my stick with a crisp *thwack* and I loved learning how to make that puck seem as if it was on a piece of string, something that's done with lots of practice and some natural ability.

My greatest natural ability was speed. I was fast on my skates, even as a little kid. I could weave and tack and glide and surge through the opponents, that puck on my stick like steel on a magnet as I raced toward the goal net to fire home the game winner. (I say "net," but more often than not it was a pair of rocks or boots on the pond with nothing but air behind them to shoot the puck through.)

As anyone who plays hockey knows, the game is about much more than stickhandling. You also have to learn to play without the puck, so you have to learn the defensive game. This means playing in your own end and backchecking. Ever notice how the puck seems to follow great players around? That's not luck. That's the result of years of studying the game.

If you don't have the puck, you'd better figure out where it's *going* to be. Otherwise you may not touch it all game.

And hockey is not for those who don't want physical contact. You know you're going to hit and get hit, so I learned how to dish them out and how to take them. When you know it's coming you kind of roll into the hit so that you go with it, not against it. That way you have a better chance of staying on your skates, snagging a loose puck, and making a play. And you're much safer right up against the boards than you are a few feet out. If you can distribute the contact evenly along the boards, you'll be in control. But if you're flying through the air, you'll be in for an awkward landing.

In those days we didn't have helmets, or visors, or mouth-guards. And since we were all at risk, we didn't hit other players to hurt them. It was rare that anyone got injured by a good clean check. We respected each other. In fact, it wasn't until I played in the NHL, in a game against Chicago in 1961, that I lost any teeth—two of them, when I was butt-ended in the mouth by Eric Nesterenko.

Of course, it wasn't always cold enough to play outdoor hockey. That's when we played street hockey . . .

I went to two elementary schools in Fredericton—first Smythe Street School, just two and a half blocks from my house, then, for grades seven and eight, York Street School, two and a half blocks in the other direction. Both are closed now, and the latter has been converted into condos.

My favorite subjects were social studies, because I liked learning about the world, and mathematics, because I could see how numbers were a kind of language when you got the hang of them. Speaking of language, I wasn't good at spelling and consider spell-check one of the greatest inventions of humankind.

Out of all those years my favorite teacher was Mrs. Smith, who taught me in grade three. She was a very nice lady, very motherly toward us, and she loved teaching. I didn't realize it at the time, but I learned a lot about how to talk to students from how she spoke to us. She was really interested in what we thought. Kids know when adults are listening and when they're just pretending to listen. She was the real deal.

I also remember a couple of principals, Mr. Close and Mr. Clowater, but those memories are painful. Today kids resolve conflict by talking to each other about it, but when I was at school, problems were resolved in the principal's office the old-fashioned way. It was pretty harsh justice, and to me, not justice at all. I was sent to the office once for leaving the playground without permission—I don't remember why, I'd probably gone after an errant ball—and another time for making jokes in the classroom, and another time for fighting back against a bully. The kid hadn't been picking on me but on the little kids, so I'd stepped in and told him to pick on someone his own size. "Or else?" he said, and my answer was to pop him in the nose. Then I had to answer for it.

When you went to the principal's office, you knew what was about to happen. You were going to get the strap—a big, tough piece of leather that the principal would whack down on your hand. (I'd try to pull my hand back just before the strap hit so that the principal would have to do it again.) If the offense was serious enough—like maybe you'd given some sass back—he'd strap you twice. That hurt. And afterward he wouldn't try to shake your throbbing hand to show what a good fellow he was even though he'd just deliberately injured a child; he'd just say, "Get out of here and I don't want to see you back again." I'm glad we've moved past that barbaric way of dealing with problems in schools. Or at least, most schools have. In the U.S., there are still nineteen states that allow corporal punishment, including spanking, paddling, and strapping. Most of these schools, no surprise to me, are in the South.

When I wasn't getting in trouble, I was being holy—but I still got in trouble. I've spoken of Michael Coster, one of my best pals in those days; we played baseball together and he lived on my street, seven houses away. Sometimes Mike and I would go to our church, St. Anne's Anglican, and sit in the back pew and kind of giggle during the service. Mike's father would give us heck. Not only was it bad manners for the minister's son to be laughing during church, it was just as bad that we were laughing while Mike's dad was trying to work.

The craziest thing Mike and I ever did was when we were ten or eleven. The two of us went out right in front of Mike's house and lay down on the busy street, our hands behind our heads, just relaxing, cars honking away at us as if to wake the dead, which was part of our plan. Mike's dad came flying out of the house when he heard all the noise. "What the H are you kids doing?" he shouted, sounding both angry and scared. We explained that we wanted to know what it felt like to be dead. Even the minister had to laugh at that one.

That same street figured into my life the only time the police were called. We used to play baseball in the middle of the road, and on this one occasion, even though we hadn't broken any windows, the neighbors called in a complaint. When the police came we hid; once they'd gone we came out and played ball again; then the police came back. When they told us we had to stop because there'd been complaints, we were quite bold in telling them that there'd been only one complaint, and that they didn't like us just because we were kids. The police laughed then, and told us that to keep the peace we should play down at the park.

The one time the police *should* have been called, they weren't. There used to be this old guy named Sam who traveled the streets of Fredericton buying beer bottles. The big ones were worth three cents, the little ones a penny. Sam had a horse and a red wagon and a bell; you'd see him coming. So my friends and I would gather some bottles and then hail Sam. He would get down from his wagon, and while some of us were selling him the bottles, the others would run around behind his wagon and steal some of the ones he already had. Sam wouldn't see a thing; he'd just give us our money and drive off. Then we'd dash over to the next block, hail him again, and sell him back his own bottles. It seems a terrible thing to have done now, but we were just having fun and making a bit of money.

So when I went to church on Sundays, I had some forgiveness to ask for. And when I was a kid in the 1930s and early 40s, our old neighborhood church, now called St. Anne's Chapel of Ease, was where my mother and sister Betty and I would go. I already spent a lot more time with my mother than my father, but on Sunday mornings we were together a lot.

I used to go to Sunday school, and I sang in the choir—until my voice changed—and I was an altar boy as well. I loved being up on the altar in that beautiful stone church, lighting the candles and swinging the incense and helping the priest perform the mass. I loved it so much that some Sundays I'd be there twice—at the communion service at eight a.m. and then again at the choir service at eleven a.m.

I still go to church today, especially when I'm back home in Fredericton. On my last visit I went twice on a Sunday—to the Catholic church with my friend Junior, and then to the Anglican church. I like being there, thinking about life, and why we're here, and what it all means. My answer to that last question is something I'm still working on.

My father would sometimes go to church with us, but most often he'd stay home and consider the world and his place in it on the living room sofa with the newspaper. It was when we got back from church that Sunday became a family day. My brother Richard was married and living in Barker's Point, but we used to get together on Saturdays and buy things at the local market for our Sunday feast.

What we didn't get from the market we got from our garden, which was a good size. I considered it partly my turf because I certainly worked it with my dad, helping him plow it and then tending it during the week. We'd grow corn, tomatoes, cucumbers, onions, lettuce, radish, and rhubarb. I knew what I had to do when I came home from school. I'd get my homework over with and then do everything in the garden that needed to be done: weeding, picking vegetables, you name it. I didn't have to be told twice. And after that, I'd play sports.

We also had a henhouse, where we kept chickens for eggs and for meat. Chicken was my favorite meal, and I used to help my dad do the slaughtering when we needed one for Sunday dinner. Killing a chicken didn't bother me; the biggest challenge was catching it: they're fast when they're trying to escape a predator, which would be me with an axe. When you caught one, you'd put its head on the chopping block and then you'd take the axe, striking clean and true on the chicken's neck so that it didn't have a head anymore. (It sounds pretty gruesome, but it's the most humane way to do it.) Then we'd dunk the headless chicken in a pot of boiling water to loosen its feathers for plucking. My father would take care of the rest, like taking out the liver and heart and cleaning the innards, before my mom actually cooked it. The experience made me connect to the food chain in a way that is still with me. You learn about life when you kill your own food.

My favorite day of the week was Saturday, though. Every Saturday night my mom would bake brown bread and make a big pot of brown beans. She also used to make boiled cabbage and corned beef, and my dad loved baked pork chops. I'd eat whatever was on the table. I had an athlete's appetite, but I don't remember ever being hungry. But on Saturdays in winter, all I wanted to do was get dinner inside me. For on those nights, I had a pressing appointment with the radio.

Since TV didn't exist when I was young, the radio was how we engaged in the wider world. And on Saturdays, the wider world meant *Hockey Night in Canada.* I was dying to hear what my hero Maurice "Rocket" Richard was doing for the Montreal Canadiens. Rocket Richard was, to me, a hero's hero. A member of eight Stanley Cup championship teams, he was a fourteen-time All-Star player, and he was fast—that's why he was called the Rocket. He showed me—well, Foster Hewitt's voice told me—what speed could do for a team: win. When the Rocket retired, he was the highest-goal-scoring player so far in pro hockey.

Foster Hewitt, as the voice behind the games, did about as much for the game as any star player. He made every Saturday night special for a hockey-crazed kid in Fredericton. And not just me. Hewitt made Saturday night magical for "hockey fans in Canada and the United States and Newfoundland," who, just like the O'Rees of Charlotte Street, would gather around their radios to listen to Hewitt paint us a picture of our favorite teams and our favorite players.

He was the guy who created and defined hockey broadcasting. Although he'd started out in the early 1920s as a sportswriter for the *Toronto Daily Star,* his sports savvy helped make him the voice of hockey. When he began announcing games on the radio in 1923, his high-pitched nasal voice made famous that phrase *"He shoots! He scores!"* And his voice would crackle when he got excited or rise when he had to shout over the roaring crowd—it was all so exciting and dramatic.

Hewitt created such wonderful pictures of the Rocket blasting in on some poor goalie that those games seemed as if they were taking place right out back on the rink in our yard. I never dreamed at the time that one day I'd be on *Hockey Night in Canada* myself. As a player.

Kids today probably watch their heroes on highlight reels and YouTube more than any other way. But I never once *watched* the Rocket. His legendary rushes and fiery intensity came to life in my imagination so vividly that I remember them as if I'd been right there in the Forum in Montreal to see them. Those epic games played out entirely in my mind.

I sometimes wonder whether my life would have been different, or somehow felt different, if I'd grown up watching Richard and other NHLers on television. That is, if I saw what they looked like. I never saw the red, white, and blue of the Habs sweaters, but I also never saw black and white— because it wasn't there for me to see. All I ever imagined as a kid was the game itself. The question of color was never part of it. It's interesting to think that the tradition of *Hockey Night in Canada* on the family radio, which was so much a part of Canadians' lives back then, allowed me to imagine a version of the game that had a place for a player like me.

———

I even learned that black people had played hockey in Canada for quite a while—ever since the late 1800s, in fact.

By that time Canada's Maritime provinces had significant black populations—descendants of those who'd migrated north during the American War of Independence in the 1770s, as my ancestor Paris O'Ree did, or of those who'd escaped slavery during the American Civil War in the 1860s. And yet, when the Halifax City Hockey League (HCHL) was formed in 1894, it was for whites only. There was, in some circles, a pseudoscientific theory that black people had weak ankles and no aptitude for the game. Therefore, why would we want to play?

So the next year, 1895, Henry Sylvester Williams, a Trinidadian law student at Halifax's Dalhousie University, joined forces with Pastor James Borden of the Dartmouth Lake Baptist Church to create the Coloured Hockey League (CHL), whose founding teams were the Halifax Eurekas, the Halifax Stanleys, and the Dartmouth Jubilees. ("Colored" was considered an acceptable term for black people right up until the mid-1960s.) Its formation was a way to encourage black youth to go to church (games happened after Sunday services), and black identity was very much part of the league.

In March 1899 the Halifax Eurekas played an exhibition game against the HCHL's Dartmouth Chebuctos, an all-white team. The Eurekas won the game 9 to 7 in the first recorded instance of interracial hockey, as it were. Black people could not only play hockey, but they could play it well enough to beat a pretty good team of white players.

The Colored Hockey League grew, and in 1900 expanded to include the Africville Sea-Sides, Hammond Plains Moss Backs, Truro Victorias/Sheiks, Amherst Royals, and Charlottetown West End Rangers of Prince Edward Island. Now it was called the Coloured Hockey League of the Maritimes (CHLM). (Meanwhile, Ontario, for example, didn't have separate black and white leagues. Hipple "Hippo" Galloway played for the Woodstock team in the Central Ontario Hockey Association, and Charley Lightfoot played for Stratford. But eventually Galloway, who also played baseball, left the game to barnstorm with a black baseball team—after an American player on his otherwise all-white baseball team objected to his presence.)

The CHLM took on new leadership at the hands of A.R. Kinney, a businessman, and James Robinson Johnston, a lawyer. The league was organized on a "challenge cup system," where the previous winner retained the title of league champion unless another team vied for it and won. The business and law connections of Kinney and Johnston attracted other successful black managers—and press coverage. White reporters loved the fast, physical play and the innovations the CHLM introduced, such as a goaltender dropping to his knees to stop a puck (that would be Henry "Braces" Franklyn of the Dartmouth Jubilees) and an early form of the slapshot (thanks to Eddie Martin of the Halifax Eurekas). These plays hadn't yet been allowed or even imagined in the white leagues. So, during the CHLM's golden years, from 1900 to 1905, its games often drew greater attendance numbers than white league games: between twelve hundred and fifteen hundred spectators, both black and white.

But even though the league was popular and its players talented, the black teams couldn't challenge for the Stanley Cup. Once Lord Stanley had donated his silver jug as hockey's championship trophy in 1893, teams could challenge the Cup holder to try to win it. The champions held the Cup until they lost their league title to another club, or until a champion from another league issued a formal challenge and subsequently defeated them in a special game or series. Some seasons saw the Cup change owners several times. Now, there was nothing in this Stanley Cup challenge that prevented black teams from participating—except for the segregation already in place: the Coloured League had to begin its season *after* the white leagues had finished theirs. In other words, it was the only league playing.

So the players didn't stay in the black leagues out of preference. If they wanted to play the game they loved at the highest level, they stayed out of necessity.

All my knowledge about people despising you because of the color of your skin, whether in hockey or in life, was to come later. When I was a little boy, all I knew was that hockey *was* my life, and that "black" meant the puck and "white" meant the ice. The only color that mattered then was silver: we all wanted to win the Stanley Cup, and we won it a thousand times on those rinks of childhood.

I played hockey because I couldn't imagine what life would

be like if I didn't play it. I believed I'd be squandering my talents if I didn't get myself out on the ice to do my thing. The game was the reason I was put on earth, and nothing was going to stop me from playing it.

Hockey would take me far from home and onto the brightest professional stage the game knows. It would give me a home, feed my family, and win me friends. It would give me some of my happiest and saddest moments. Most importantly, it made me proud of who I am and what I do. And it made my dreams come true. So that's where the next part of my story begins.

3.

RAISING MY GAME

You might say that I owe my hockey career to a broken collarbone. It happened during my first year at Fredericton High School, after I'd joined the school's team. The coach's son was playing on it too, which can sometimes be a problem, depending on the coach. This time it was a problem.

I was on the ice and the coach's son was skating toward me with the puck. He had his head down. The first thing you learn after you've mastered skating: keep your head up! Anyway, as he was admiring his skates, I stepped into him, knocking him to the ice and, as it turned out, breaking his collarbone. The coach was very upset, telling me that this wasn't the way hockey was played at Fredericton High School. Just like that, I was off the team.

I was disappointed, of course, but it was getting kicked off the team that directed me to the path that would take me to the pros. By the time I was fifteen I was playing for the Fredericton Falcons in the New Brunswick Amateur Hockey Association. I was playing hockey all the time—and when I wasn't, I was thinking it and dreaming it or listening to it on the radio. And, of course, I was trying to keep up with my schoolwork, which became more challenging as the years went on. Mainly because my head was on the ice. If you grew up playing hockey, you know what I mean. There's just no way school can capture your imagination the way hockey does. I'm not saying that's a good thing. School is important! But the reality is, for some people, hockey is just about the most exciting thing in the world. You live and breathe it. You think about it all the time: things you'd like to try, things you'd do differently, things you might improve. And then there's just daydreaming. It takes a lot of work to focus on something other than hockey when you love it as much as many of us do.

Over the next three years I moved on up through the Fredericton hockey system. (The Maritimes' segregation in ice hockey at the turn of the twentieth century had gone by the time I was ready to play. In fact, Manny McIntyre, a black player who'd become famous as part of an all-black line in Quebec, was born in Fredericton in 1918 and played high school hockey there.) In 1951–52 I played with the Fredericton Merchants of the York County Hockey League, followed by three games with the Fredericton Capitals of the New Brunswick Senior Hockey League. We were young players and I was one of the youngest, but we were keen and had a taste for winning.

After a season with the Junior Capitals, I made a step up to the senior ranks for a full season in 1953–54. That year we won both the New Brunswick Senior Hockey League championship and the Maritimes Senior Playoffs. We also played in the Eastern Canada Allan Cup tournament—an exciting prospect for me, but I knew it was important to show all I had and all I can do. You could say I was used to proving myself in every game I played. As it turned out, I scored seven goals in seven games. So I was sad when the Capitals lost the semifinal. (Making matters worse, at the same time the team I loved, the Canadiens, and my hero Rocket Richard lost the Stanley Cup to the driven, hard-playing Detroit Red Wings.)

I was close to Robbie Miles and Tim Bliss, who were my linemates. With me playing left wing, Robbie center, and Tim right wing, we just gelled. I was the youngest of the three but the most aggressive. Now, I've always wanted to win every period of every game I've played. Other teams don't always love playing against guys like that. Sparks do fly. Some guys like to take a shift off now and then, and they don't always appreciate a guy who plays hard until the whistle goes. But I've never met a player who doesn't value a guy like that on his own team.

When I was little and played hockey it was just me on the ice, with help from Coot, my big brother. And, of course, my parents came to every game. But when I was in my teens I also played with my friend Junior, an excellent baseball player as well as a hockey player, and our friend Walter "Bubsy" Mills, who could play any sport you put in front of him. His first time on the court as a high school basketball player, for example, saw him named the tournament's most valuable player. With his stocky frame, he was also a star fullback and linebacker in football, and a guy you wanted on your team on the ice.

There's a great story that captures the free spirit and fine athlete that was Bubsy. In one hockey game he played in against my high school, we went into sudden-death overtime: Bubsy's favorite place to be. He begged the coach to put him on the ice so that he could score the winning goal. The coach didn't listen—Bubsy's pleas sounded to him like just swagger—but the game went on, and finally Bubsy got his ice time. He skated right over to the Fredericton High bench and told the players they could take off their skates because he was going to end the game with his next shot. When the ref dropped the puck for the faceoff, the center passed the puck back to Bubsy and he charged across the ice, beat one guy, then beat another, and then put the puck in the net. Game over—and it was Bubsy who'd won it.

It was Coot, though, who remained my best hockey coach as I was coming up through the ranks. He was in his early thirties at the time, a solid five ten and over two hundred pounds. Coot played defense but would never use his stick on guys. He played the body every time. On several occasions when we were practicing together, Coot would bodycheck me hard to the ice. So hard, in fact, that it would bring tears to my eyes. I asked him, "My goodness, brother, why did you do that?"

He was as blunt as his check. "You're going to get hit in the big league, brother, so you'd better *learn* how to get hit."

He was right, and so I learned. I was always prepared to take a blow as well as to give a good clean hit when I saw the chance. And during my hockey career I gave, and got, a lot of hits.

Even though the Fredericton Capitals were semipro, I couldn't actually get paid for playing for them since it would have ruined my amateur standing at school for other sports. They did, though, give me money for travel and meals when the team was on the road.

The funny thing was that when my high school coach— the one who'd kicked me off the team—saw me playing with the Capitals, he wanted me to come back to play. I said no. He'd had his chance—and he hadn't given me a chance.

But I got my revenge on him at the York Arena. Back in 1947, when it opened, the arena was Fredericton's big new covered hockey rink. In fact it was so big for its time, and there was so much snow in winter, that the roof had to be shoveled after every snowfall. The fear was that the weight of the snow would bring the roof down. Of course, that didn't worry me because I wasn't thinking snow, I was thinking ice. Some nights I'd even sleep there so that I could get on the ice really early the next day and have it all to myself as I did my hockey drills. You might say, with some understatement, that

I was a rink rat. That arena was my second home: not only did I practice and play there, but I did odd jobs around the place for pocket money.

One day I was sweeping the bleachers when Fredericton High's hockey team showed up for a game against another high school. They were beating them pretty badly, so at the end of second period I said to the other school, "Looks like you guys could use some help." They said they sure could, as they were depleted by injuries and knew that I played for the Capitals. So I suited up for them, came out in third period, and scored five goals. "We" wound up beating Fredericton High. It was a sweet moment, with its coach once again regretting his hotheaded decision to kick me off the team.

Hockey and sports in general were my life in those days. I didn't have girlfriends as a teenager because there weren't that many black girls at school, and even though Fredericton was pretty tolerant, it wasn't done for a black boy to be seen with a white girl. My parents had always said, "Stick to your own kind" to avoid trouble. I never quite saw how love could be trouble, but I did know that other people didn't see love when they saw two people of different colors together. As I often say, we're all part of the human race, and so race has no place in how we see one another. How a person lives and behaves and treats his or her fellow humans does. But I know not everyone sees things that way.

Back in high school I had crushes on girls who played sports, but I kept them to myself. Nor did I take girls to the movies. Instead I'd go with my friends, sneaking out with Junior at night or going to Saturday matinees. We were all crazy about westerns.

There were two movie theaters: the Capitol at the corner of Regent and King and the Gaiety on Queen Street. The Capitol played westerns while the Gaiety showed more love stories, so we always went to the Capitol. It cost a dime to see a movie and a nickel for popcorn, meaning you could see a double feature for a quarter. My favorites were *The Durango Kid* and *The Red Ryder* and the Little Beaver series. I still love westerns and watch them as often as I can. To this day Junior will call to tell me that *The Wild Bunch* is on TV. Since he lives in New Jersey and I live in San Diego, that gives me a three-hour heads-up to find out when it'll be screening in my house. And I'll watch it again. It's one of my absolute favorites, as is *The Big Country*. Gregory Peck, one of the greatest actors who ever took to the silver screen, is superb in that film.

My friends and I also fancied ourselves as cowboys. Out on the end of the Woodstock Road was a riding stable run by Mrs. Goodein, a no-nonsense woman to whom we gave a lot of nonsense. I loved going out there with Junior and Bubsy to rent horses. Once we reached the top of the hill, away from the stables, the landscape would level out—and that's when we'd dig our heels into the sides of our horses, yell "Giddyup," and gallop off as fast as we could.

Which was, of course, strictly forbidden. So Mrs. Goodein started sending a minder up with us to make sure we just walked our horses. But once we got to the plateau, Bubsy would cough—and that was our signal to take off in all directions. The minder could follow only one of us, so we'd beat the system that way. Mrs. Goodein would tell us not to gallop the horses every time, we'd promise not to every time, and she'd rent them to us all the same, knowing full well we were likely to break that promise.

One of the scariest—and in retrospect funniest—outings we had happened when Junior and I came around a corner and saw Bubsy's horse but no Bubsy. We called out: no answer. We couldn't figure out where he'd gone, or if aliens had snatched him or what. As I sat on my saddle under a tree, thinking about it, Bubsy leapt down from a branch and onto my horse, startling the hell out of us both. Off we galloped, until I could finally get that poor horse back under control.

I was what you might call a natural athlete and played practically every sport I could. I came second in a tennis tournament and was a pretty good gymnast, winning some meets; I was also a baseball player and a varsity rugby player. In fact, in 1953 Fredericton High beat St. John's in the provincial high school rugby tournament. The score was 12–5 for us, and I scored seven of those points, including a pretty fine forty-yard penalty kick.

I also ran track. Junior ran it too, but he could never beat me, although he did make second place a few times. In fact, a few years ago he found a photo of us running track, with me winning and him running second. He fiddled with it a bit (he's an engineer) and produced a new photo that had him winning and me in second. When he showed it to me I thought he'd actually won a race off me, but then, true to my competitive nature, I remembered all my victories—along with who beat whom when I didn't win—and I knew, just as surely as the sun rises in the east, that Junior never did beat me in a foot race. We had a good laugh over his fake news.

My athletic ability in high school gave me confidence—I felt like I could do anything I wanted to do. And that confidence allowed me not only to say no to the high school coach but also to cross my first color barrier. I was just thirteen.

Even though Fredericton was a pretty tolerant city, there were still places where a black person couldn't go. For instance, a black person wouldn't go into a white barbershop to have his hair cut. There weren't signs up or anything like that—we just knew. And I knew it was wrong. Now, this is an odd thing, as there wasn't racism of the kind that I would come to know when I made my first trip to the American South, but we understood the possible perils of stepping across a line no one acknowledged was there. It wasn't that we were segregated. But we weren't integrated, either. We all lived with an unspoken code. It wasn't clear what would happen if you broke it, but there was a strong feeling that it shouldn't be broken. Just as you wouldn't, as a guy, walk into the ladies' room to use the facilities, I, as a black kid, wouldn't go into a white barbershop. Instead I would go out to Barker's Point, where the black families lived, and go to a barber there.

But then one day I did things differently. Five houses down from us, on the same side of the street, lived a family called

McQuade. I was friends with their son, and Joe, his father, who was a barber, would cut my hair on their porch. We became very good friends. When I used to walk by the shop where Mr. McQuade worked, I'd wave to him and he'd wave back. So one day I asked him what would happen if I came into his shop to have him cut my hair. He paused, looked me in the eye, and said, "I don't know. I haven't given it any thought. Why don't you give it a try?"

The O'Ree family was well respected in Fredericton. And since my brothers and sisters were very good in sports, as was I, we were well known, too. So when I walked into Joe McQuade's barbershop, heads turned because it was me— and because it was *me*.

The four barber chairs were occupied, with a couple of people waiting. I sat down and Joe nodded at me, but when it was my turn he was occupied. The next barber looked at me suspiciously. "I'm waiting for Mr. McQuade," I told him. No one said a word to me. Then, when Joe was finished with his customer, he turned and said, "I'm ready for you now, Willie," and proceeded to cut my hair. I knew what was going on, but I wasn't nervous.

After that, I continued getting my hair cut at the barbershop. I knew Joe McQuade got some flak for it from the city's bigots, but I kept going and he kept cutting my hair. Then, once he'd retired, he went back to cutting my hair at his house.

Although it may seem like a small thing, for me it was huge. I was just a teenager, but it showed me that I could change things if I tried. My parents worried that I'd bring trouble onto myself because of color, but I figured trouble was happening because of color already. I wasn't going to let it stop me. I knew then that I could play hockey with the big guys. I also knew that there hadn't yet been a black man who played pro in the NHL, even though black humans had been playing hockey for as long as white humans had. My young eyes were seeing how the world around me worked.

I knew I needed a winning team if I were to fulfill my dream of winning in the NHL. Seems simple enough, but if I wanted to raise the level of my game, I couldn't do it in New Brunswick. And if I wanted to make it to the pros, I pretty much had to play in the junior league.

When I was nineteen I received an offer to play junior hockey with the Quebec Frontenacs in the province's Junior A Hockey League. Quebec City is almost four hundred miles northwest of Fredericton, and when you're nineteen, that's a very long way. But the Frontenacs' coach was Phil Watson, who'd been a mighty right-winger, playing thirteen seasons in the six-team NHL—twelve of them for the New York Rangers, where he'd won a Stanley Cup in 1940, and one for the Montreal Canadiens, where he'd won another Cup in 1944. So I was flattered that such a team would want me, but felt skittish about leaving home.

My friend Bob Mabie—who'd go on to a long hockey career at the University of St. Thomas—had been invited to Quebec as well. He said we should give it a try, and that if we didn't like it we could just come back. That's what I told my parents as well. They knew I wanted to be a professional ath-lete, and that if you wanted to be a pro hockey player in those days, you had to play junior hockey. Today you can go to college, on a scholarship if you're good, and get into the NHL that way. But back then there was only one route to the show.

So my parents gave me their blessing, and with butterflies in my stomach, off I went to Quebec City. Bob and I both roomed with the Begin family. As it turned out, Monsieur Begin was a butcher, meaning we had a lot of steak on the table, which was more than fine with me. I'll eat almost any-thing, and while my favorite food is chicken, steak runs a close second. Another advantage was that the Begins lived close to where the Frontenacs played: the Colisée, a big arena with a barrel-vault roof, built in 1949 to seat over ten thou-sand very devoted Quebec City hockey fans.

It's an old city as far as our young country goes, with more to see and do—and eat—than a nineteen-year-old from the Maritimes could imagine. In fact, Quebec City is one of the oldest cities in North America, founded as it was—or settled is maybe the better term—in 1608, when Samuel de Champlain arrived and set up camp on an abandoned Algonquin set-tlement. There the French built high stone walls and a fort called La Citadelle; they still stand today, the oldest city forti-fications in existence in North America. And when you pass under the Porte St. Louis or Porte St. Jean gates, you leave modern Quebec City and enter the old town, where I would love to go for crepes and cider.

In 1759 a famous battle was fought on the Plains of Abraham, just outside the city. And even though the British defeated the French, when I lived there the overwhelming majority of people spoke French as their mother tongue. I knew some French because I'd taken it in school, so I could get by. And playing hockey, whether in English or French, was still hockey.

When I first started playing hockey at a high level, my parents, Harry and Rosebud, worried that, as a black player in a white world, I'd get hurt. After all, hockey players have an infinite number of ways of settling scores. If they don't want you there, you'll know it—and it's going to be painful. But I wasn't worried about that. In fact, I wasn't worried about anything. I knew I was good. And I had a dream of making the NHL—of becoming what Phil Watson told me I could be when I played for him in that 1954–55 season on the Quebec Frontenacs. He said that, if I wanted it badly enough, I had the skills to make the National Hockey League. I was thrilled by his assessment of my hockey talents. Given his background, this was, I reckoned, someone who knew what he was talking about.

Phil Watson also said that I could be "the Jackie Robinson of hockey," another idea that filled my heart with hope and fueled my ambition. For when Jackie Robinson became the first black man to suit up for a Major League Baseball team on April 15, 1947, he broke the MLB color barrier. There'd been Negro League baseball for decades, with some of the best players in the game to be found in their ranks. But they couldn't break free from those ranks, which held them back just like the chains that had held back their ancestors. And Jackie Robinson not only broke those chains when he started at first base for the Brooklyn Dodgers—he also won the Rookie of the Year award and was an All-Star for six seasons.

Robinson had played in Montreal for the Royals, the Brooklyn Dodgers' farm team. People in Montreal loved him, but when he made it to the major leagues in 1947, it was very much the case that, because he was black, players in the league did not. Pitchers threw balls at his head. Fans lobbed other things at him. One of his own Brooklyn Dodgers teammates started a petition demanding that he be kicked off the team. And when he played against Southern teams, the Ku Klux Klan issued death threats from behind their white hoods.

Jackie Robinson just played ball, and he was the best. Such was his greatness as a man and as a player that MLB retired his number, 42, across the entire league, forever. The only other time that honor has been given to a player by any major league sport was in 2000, when the NHL retired the jersey of a skinny kid from Brampton, Ontario, by the name of Gretzky.

In one of those coincidences that we could also call fate, I met Jackie Robinson in 1949, when I was thirteen years old. My baseball team, the West Enders, had won Fredericton's bantam city championship, and were rewarded with a trip to New York City to see the Brooklyn Dodgers play.

We drove down in five or six cars with our sponsors and became tourists. After the Empire State Building—which hurt my neck to look at, I had to lean so far back—we saw Radio City Music Hall. Then we crossed over the Brooklyn

Bridge to Ebbets Field to watch Robinson work his magic. I don't remember who they played or even if the Dodgers won that day. All I remember is the greatness of Jackie Robinson. He was fast, he was calm, and his every play was as if he'd invented baseball.

After the game we gathered in the Dodgers' dugout and met Robinson himself. He could not have been nicer, asking each of us our name and whether we liked baseball. When my turn came, I told him that I liked baseball a lot but that I liked hockey more. He looked surprised and said that hockey didn't have any black players. I told him he was looking at one, and that he'd see me make my mark on the game the way he'd made his on baseball.

Sure, one might think, here's a kid who doesn't know anything of the world, dreaming big dreams that'll just vanish in the ether of adulthood. But I knew I was good.

It wasn't just Phil Watson who'd told me I was NHL material. So too did my next coach, Black Jack Stewart, when I moved west to play for the Junior A Kitchener Canucks in 1955–56. I'd since become the property of the Montreal Canadiens as in those days, teams just moved players around like checkers on a board and you had no say in it whatsoever, so one day Watson told me that the Habs had moved me to their team in Kitchener. If you didn't go you wouldn't play, and so I went—and made the same impression on Stewart as I had on Watson. "You're good enough to make the NHL, Willie" is what he told me, and I was sure that his twelve seasons in the NHL and his two Stanley Cup rings couldn't be wrong either.

In Kitchener I was having one of those seasons that players dream about. We had a forty-eight-game schedule, and by game 41 I'd already scored thirty goals and added twenty-eight assists to give me fifty-eight points. I was tenth in the league when it came to goal scoring that season. So in November, when we played away against the Guelph Biltmores, our rivals in the Ontario Hockey Association, I was looking to add to that number to get the attention of NHL scouts.

But it was on that night that I had to begin everything all over again.

4.

THE INJURY

Every athlete knows that one injury can spell the end of a career, and every athlete does their best to prevent that injury from happening. You train hard, you take care to warm up and cool down, and you treat your body with the utmost respect because it's the vehicle through which you play your sport. But there are some things you can't control, and on November 22, 1955, I was going to literally come face to face with one of them when we played against the Guelph Biltmores.

Guelph and Kitchener-Waterloo are close, separated by just twenty-five miles. Guelph is an old city in southwestern Ontario, always known to be a clean, safe place where a steady flow of manufacturing jobs maintained its good reputation and grew hockey fans. Kitchener and Waterloo are even older twin cities, with Kitchener's name having been changed from

Berlin in 1916 on account of the anti-German feeling that spread through Canada during the First World War.

Their two teams were pretty equal as well, jockeying in the standings to eventually finish the season tied with fifty-three points. I knew it was going to be a tough game, especially with the playoffs coming up fast. Only seven games were left in our season.

We got a power play early in the first period. I was on the ice, trying to add to my goal total and get our team out front. I skated the puck deep into the Guelph zone along the left wing, then passed it back to my teammate Kent Douglas on the blue line. Then I skated over to stand in front of the Guelph goalie, trying to screen him when Kent took his shot. Maybe I'd get the tip of my stick on the puck and deflect it into the net.

Kent, who'd go on to become one of the NHL's fiercest shooters with the Toronto Maple Leafs, fired one of his thundering slapshots. Just when I heard the puck crack off his stick I was cross-checked from behind by a Guelph defenseman. Then, as my head spun toward Kent's shot, the puck deflected off the stick of another player and right into my face.

That's all I remember. The rest I had to read about in the newspapers, and it's difficult to read it even today.

The puck struck my face with such force that it broke my nose, crushed my right cheekbone, and almost pulverized the retina in my right eye. NHLers can shoot the puck around a hundred miles per hour. I have no idea how hard Kent shot the puck that day, but it felt as though he'd hit me in the face with a baseball bat. I was down on the ice lying in a pool of my own blood.

The ambulance took to me Kitchener-Waterloo hospital. The next day the newspapers reported that my condition was "fair" and that the attending physician, Dr. H.R. Henderson Sr., an eye specialist, said that my right eye had "suffered some damage, but the full extent of the injury has not yet been determined." And stitches had closed up a deep cut to my right eyelid.

From where I lay, things, shall we say, "looked" a lot worse. I couldn't see out of my right eye because of the bandage covering it. But I couldn't see out of my left eye, either, having blinked so hard and so fast in panic to relieve what in those days they called "hysterical blindness." For a frightening while, my left eye had gone blind, too, in a kind of psychological sympathy with my right eye.

Dr. Henderson was more direct with me than he'd been with the newspapers. "Willie," he said, "the puck has destroyed about 95 percent of your right eye. You will not ever be able to see out of it again, and you won't be able to play hockey ever again either. I'm sorry."

He *was* sorry. I was devastated, but I'll always be grateful to Dr. Henderson for not telling anyone else what he told me. Because during the next four days I spent in the hospital, I made up my mind that I would play hockey again. I just wouldn't tell anyone about my blind right eye.

Well, I wouldn't tell anyone but my sister Betty, with whom I was very close in both age and temperament. When I came home from the hospital, she thought, as did our parents, that I was healed and fit to play. Instead I was learning how to fake it as a one-eyed nineteen-year-old hockey player.

I told Betty the truth because I felt that at least one other person had to know, and she was the one I trusted most. She was alarmed, but she promised to keep it a secret. Betty knew how much playing hockey meant to me, and she knew that if our parents found out, my hockey days would be over. And true to her word, she never told a soul. In fact, my friend Junior didn't know about it until seven or eight years ago. When we O'Rees want to keep a secret, we can do it.

My bigger problem was the fact that I played left wing, which meant that when I was flying down the ice with the puck— my good eye closest to the boards, my blind eye closest to the rink—I'd need to have my head on a complete swivel to see whether anyone was coming to hit me.

So I spent that winter in my own private rehab. And as I skated I began to get a feel for the ice as a one-eyed player. I knew I could adapt when I stepped back onto the ice for Kitchener the next season. My left eye wasn't noticeably better in terms of compensating for my blind right eye, but I think it probably was, since to this day I'm still 20/20 in my left eye. Plus I was still fast, and I could still play the game. This was a huge relief to me, even though I knew that if a puck ever hit me in my left eye, that would be the end.

It was a chance I had to take to make my professional dream come true. You might say I wasn't going to let a little thing like blindness stop me, but that makes it sound glib. I was scared, for sure, but I was also afraid of what my life would be like if I didn't try to make the pros. I could live with the risk to my eye, but I couldn't live with the "what ifs" if I didn't go full steam ahead with my hockey dream.

As winter gave way to spring I got back into baseball—and found that my skills on the field hadn't been affected by my blind right eye. Maybe, I thought, *this* could be the sport where I became a professional. I knew I was already good enough to play pro hockey in Fredericton. Could I play in a bigger league, on a grander stage? Or would I have to begin again and leave my hockey dreams on the baseball field? All those questions would be flooding my mind because, in the summer of 1956, major league baseball came calling for Willie O'Ree.

5.

THE SUMMER GAME

I'm very happy to be living in today's world, as I believe that we've improved as a species and that more people on our planet are better off than they were when I was born more than eighty years ago. Of course, we have a long way to go, assuming we don't destroy the planet on our journey toward perfection.

But there's one thing that I do think was better when I was growing up: how we as kids played. Our games and sports were governed by the seasons, and not so much by associations and leagues and money. And we also just loved to play, as we didn't have cell phones or computer games to turn our attention away from the field or rink. In autumn we played rugby and basketball and began the hockey season, which stretched into the winter and ended when the ice melted in spring. Then we began track and field, volleyball, tennis, and baseball, which I played onward into summer.

I played shortstop and second base because I liked to be in the hot spots—just as I played forward in hockey because I wanted to be up there in the other team's zone, putting the puck in the net, getting in the goalie's face, tussling with the opposing defensemen who were trying to get me out of there. I liked the action, and if you play shortstop or second base, you're right in the middle of it.

As a shortstop, you have to be fast—able to blast from a standing start forward or laterally—because the chance of a ground ball being hit into your defensive area is higher than that for any other player on the field. And you have to cover for second and third base if those players are playing the ball, so you're moving around a lot. As a second baseman, you have to be able to throw and to master the double play. And you have to keep your nerve as guys slide into second, trying to knock you over while you're trying to throw to first base to make that double play. So I figured I was handling two of the toughest positions on the field.

And in 1956, in the spring after my eye injury, I was playing baseball for Fredericton. That way I was able to keep my five-ten, 175-pound self in shape for hockey. And I also made a few bucks. Not a lot, but it was good to get paid to play because that's what I was: a professional athlete.

The question in my mind, though, was this: At which sport was I going to be a professional? I was playing minor pro hockey but had my eye (the left one) squarely on the NHL.

Meanwhile I'd inherited my dad's baseball talent to the point that other teams were showing interest in what I could do on the field.

Hockey is a game of constant motion, high speed, and violence; baseball is a game of long periods of waiting and short periods of motion. In hockey you can lose yourself totally in the moment because your shift is short and those three twenty-minute periods fly by, whereas in baseball you can contemplate eternity because those nine innings have no clock on them.

And since the movement in baseball is slower, I found that it was much easier than hockey to play it with one eye. You're staring straight ahead when the batter is up, and if he hits the ball to you, then you turn your entire body in the direction in which you need to throw the ball—so once again you're looking straight ahead, and not on a 180-degree swivel at some hockey player speeding in to smash you into the boards. In short, it's a much gentler game—so I had no trouble playing it with only one eye.

Proof of this came during that 1956 season when the Marysville Royals asked if I'd like to suit up for them. Today Marysville is part of Fredericton, just a few miles from the city center on the north side of the Saint John River, but in those days it was pretty rural; to me, it felt as though I'd be literally going to the farm team. Even so, they had a pretty good roster, and had won the New Brunswick Senior League championship the season before. And when they said they'd pay me more than what I was making in Fredericton, I became a Marysville Royal.

In fact, the Royals were a very good team. And I wanted to play for the best, figuring it would test me, allowing me to make the clearest decision about what sport to dedicate my life to, now that I'd reached the ripe old age of twenty.

That decision came sooner than expected when two scouts from the National League's Milwaukee Braves approached me in the dressing room after watching me play in a game. The Braves had moved to Milwaukee from Boston in 1953, after eight decades as the Boston Braves. Babe Ruth had played in Boston at the end of his great career. And Milwaukee loved the Braves. The team had been invigorated by the move, finishing second in the National League to the Brooklyn Dodgers in the 1955 season. They'd go on to win the World Series in 1957.

But now, in 1956, these two scouts had their eyes on me. "We like your prospects, Willie, and we'd like you to come down to our minor league club for a tryout," they said.

"And where is that?" I asked.

"Waycross, Georgia."

I knew how black people were treated in the southern United States, so I said, "I don't think so."

They looked surprised. They represented a very good team; I should have been flattered and thrilled by their invitation. But it was the first time in my professional sporting life that my skin color made a difference, and the difference was to me. I was very leery of doing anything in the state of Georgia, or in the American South in general.

The year before, a little league team made up of black kids in South Carolina won the state championship—because all fifty-five white teams had withdrawn rather than play against black kids. Of course, the state didn't count the black kids as the champions in the end, but it was a pretty stark comment on how racism started early in the South. And just after New Year's Day 1955, Georgia Tech threatened to pull out of the Sugar Bowl in New Orleans because their opponent, the University of Pittsburgh, had a black player, running back Bobby Grier. In the end sanity prevailed and Grier played. But those two instances of Southern racism paled when I thought about what had happened to Emmett Till.

Emmett Till had just turned fourteen in the summer of 1955 when he left his home in Chicago to spend the summer with relatives in rural Mississippi. His mother warned her "class clown" son that the kinds of things he could joke about in the North could get him into trouble in the South.

Emmett arrived in Money, Mississippi, on August 21, 1955, and stayed with his great uncle, Moses Wright, who was a sharecropper; Emmett helped him with the cotton harvest. Three days after his arrival, he and a group of other teens went to a local grocery store after work. Emmett apparently joked with the white female cashier—maybe by whistling at her or flirting with her.

Then he went back to his uncle's home, not mentioning it to him because there must have been, in his mind, nothing to mention. But in the middle of the night on August 28, the cashier's husband and his half-brother broke into Moses

Wright's home, put a gun to the terrified Emmett Till's head, and took him away.

They beat him something awful. They gouged out one of his eyes. Then they took this child to the banks of the Tallahatchie River and shot him in the head. Finally they tied his body to a large metal fan with some barbed wire and dumped poor Emmett into the river.

His uncle went to the police, and the two murderers were arrested the next day. Emmett's body was found two days later, his face unrecognizable.

Tens of thousands of people lined the streets of Chicago to pay their respect to Emmett Till and his family. His mother kept Emmett's casket open so that people could see what racists had done to her son. The black magazine *Jet* and the black newspaper *The Chicago Defender* published pictures of the boy in his casket, catching the attention of the world. Emmett's murder was one of those terrible events that fueled the rising civil rights movement.

So did the trial of the men who killed Emmett Till. Despite the fact that Emmett's uncle had identified the killers in court, an all-white male jury (black people and women couldn't serve as jurors in Mississippi back then) deliberated for little more than an hour and acquitted the killers. The following year, the two men told *Look* magazine how they had tortured and murdered Emmett, and got paid for their story.

So, you can see why a trip to the American South was not on my to-do list. My parents agreed. "Don't go," they told me. "We don't want you to get hurt."

They had also said this to me about playing hockey, but that was because of the rough-and-tumble nature of the game. Now they were saying it because they didn't want me to wind up dead in a river. I liked to joke around with people and have a laugh, but what was funny to my friends in Fredericton might be fatal to me in the Deep South.

My mother and father had grown up in Canada. They'd been able to live where they wanted, to send their kids to school where they wanted, to eat and drink and lodge where they wanted. But they remembered that the O'Rees had begun as slaves. The family had fled the southern United States and made a fine life in Canada. So why on earth would I want to go back?

Well, because I wanted to be a professional athlete. And here I was, being offered a shot at the big leagues of baseball. Was the benefit greater than the risk?

I decided to speak to Coot. I trusted him, and I would trust what he had to tell me. Like all wise men, he didn't tell me anything, but rather asked me what I wanted.

"How do *you* feel about it, Willie?"

I said I was proud that I had a chance to go to a major league camp. And that deep down I'd like to go and test myself.

And so Coot said, "If you feel in your heart and your mind that you want to go, then you should go."

I went home and explained this to my parents. They were worried about me, but I was an adult now and there wasn't a lot they could do except tell me again to be careful. Which I always was. Of course, I can imagine now, as a parent myself, how worried they must have been about me back then.

—

The Braves bought me a plane ticket to fly from Fredericton to Atlanta, which in those days meant taking a Trans-Canada Airlines plane to Montreal and changing to a TWA flight south. It was my first time on an airplane.

When I arrived at the Atlanta airport I needed to use the restroom, so I looked for one when I walked into the terminal. I had two choices: a restroom for Whites Only and another one for "Coloreds."

It's funny, but the only other time I'd made a decision in my life based on the color of my skin was to walk in and get my hair cut at Joe McQuade's barbershop, where there weren't any other black people but where it didn't matter in the end. And it was more about Fredericton's habits than it was about anything official. So maybe I was seeing two types of discrimination: one an invisible line daring me to cross; the other a wall telling me that no matter what, I wasn't going to get through.

When I look in the mirror in the morning I don't see color, I see me. I see a man. But at that very moment, I was endorsing segregation in the American South by walking into the Colored restroom. I didn't want trouble as soon as I landed. And I had received the message loud and clear: I was very much a second-class person—and to some, not a person at all—in this part of the world.

When I exited the terminal I spotted a black taxi driver. At the time, there was, in the United States, a travel guide for black people called *The Negro Travelers' Green Book*. It listed places where black people could find food and lodging, given the segregation laws and good old-fashioned racism that prevented us from being served or lodged in white establishments.

I knew that this taxi driver would be my human Green Book, and he was. He took to me to a hotel run by and for black people in Atlanta and I spent the night there, though I didn't sleep too well. I was very uncomfortable with what this place was doing to me. For the first time in my life I was being segregated because of my color. I knew I'd come to the city to test my baseball skills against the best, but I was already getting a strong sense of what the cost of this was going to be to who I was.

The next day I took the bus to Waycross, Georgia, over two hundred miles south of Atlanta—which is to say, the Deep South. Now, around that time, some southern cities and states were desegregating their buses thanks to Rosa Parks, who'd been arrested in Montgomery, Alabama, in 1955 for refusing to give her bus seat to a white man—an "illegal" act because of the city's racial segregation ordinances. In response, a young pastor at the Dexter Avenue Baptist Church named Martin Luther King, Jr. led a boycott of the Montgomery bus company that lasted a year, until the Supreme Court upheld a lower court ruling that Montgomery's segregated bus seating was, in fact, illegal. But I wasn't in Montgomery; I was on a bus to Waycross, and Georgia still had segregated seating. So I had to sit at the back of that bus for the four-hour ride.

The Braves' training camp had been built on the old Waycross Air Force Base left over from the Second World War.

The red clay that made up most of the ground surface would have been good for planes to take off from and land on, but it also stuck to our baseball cleats. And the floor of the dressing room—in reality a big, cold concrete bunker—was covered in the stuff. The camp itself was about a half-mile square and surrounded by swamp. (In the morning you'd see the mist rising off it, about a hundred yards away.) The place was used not only for spring training but also for "player evaluation" of guys like me. And it was big: it could hold between 150 and 300 players. When I finally got there and checked in, they gave me a standard gray practice uniform and a number, 14, that I had to sew on myself.

The great Hank Aaron, who broke Babe Ruth's record and retired with 755 home runs, had been at the camp in 1954. This great slugger and All-Star right-fielder, who started his pro career in 1952 in the Negro Leagues playing for the Indianapolis Clowns (yes, that was their name), said, "Other than being eaten alive by mosquitoes and shot at, Waycross was great."

The "Hammer" really was shot at in Waycross. He'd taken the camp bus into town for a haircut, but missed the bus back and had to walk. It was dark by the time he got there, so he took a shortcut through the surrounding woods and into the camp. That's when an armed guard spotted this black kid sneaking about and started shooting. Fortunately for Aaron— and the history of baseball—the guard was a lousy shot.

Aaron was there three years before me, and so he got to bunk with white guys. That's because, after the famous 1954 *Brown v. Board of Education* case had made school segregation illegal, white Southerners responded by segregating everything else, including the barracks that served as the camp's dormitories. There were six of them. Coaches, managers, scouts, and front office people slept in the first barrack; the white American players slept in the next three; the guys from Puerto Rico and the Dominican Republic slept in the fifth; and the black players like me had the sixth, which was closest to the swamp.

Still, the Braves had spent money on that camp. It was a big step up from what I knew back in New Brunswick, even if I was living in a swamp surrounded by racists.

After breakfast we'd put on our uniforms and then head outside to begin the morning calisthenics and stretching. We did infield drills and outfield drills, and they had pits where you could practice sliding. And of course there was batting practice on every one of the camp's four diamonds. These were built around a two-story brick tower that stood about thirty yards from each diamond's home plate. So as you did drills and swung at pitches, scouts and managers would sit in the tower with a bird's-eye view of the players on all four diamonds.

The camp also featured nine wooden buildings left over from the war. One served as office space for scouts, coaches, managers, and so on; another was used as a clubhouse, where three nights a week they showed movies on its TV. It had a jukebox, too, and we could relax with games—ping pong, shuffleboard, horseshoe pits. I made friends with some of the black players from the Deep South: one from Atlanta, a couple from Mississippi. I told them that although we had racism and prejudice in Canada, things weren't as bad as they were here—and when I told them that most of my friends were white they were astonished. Still, it made my point. Curfew was set at eleven p.m., but there was no Junior Doherty with a ladder to help me escape from this place.

During the first three weeks we worked out in the morning and then played games in the afternoon, mostly against teams made up of guys in the camp, but sometimes against other teams training in Georgia. I played shortstop and second base, just as I did back home. The first week was all right. The next week we played an exhibition game and I got a couple of hits, but what was new to me were the racial jeers from the white players, both in the camp and on outside teams. I let it go in one ear and out the other, but I'd never experienced anything like that from my hockey player teammates in Canada.

On the first Sunday we were there I went into town with some of the other black players to a black Baptist church. St. Peter's Missionary was just a little place, with a piano instead of an organ like my church back home. The service was much simpler than what I'd grown up with, too, much more emotionally direct and musically vital, with the rhythms of African American life in the Deep South driving the hymns. I'd never experienced anything like it. But it was comforting to be among black Christians praying together in this hostile part of the world. I felt my kinship with these fellow Christians keenly.

And yet, especially combined with my new experience of segregation, it showed me something I hadn't considered before. The way I'd grown up, there weren't two ways of doing things—black and white—and certainly not at church. It had never occurred to me that skin color had anything to do with religion. Why would it? But now, among people I considered my brothers and sisters, and who saw me the same way, I had to ask myself whether St. Anne's and its liturgy would somehow be less *mine* now that I'd worshipped with people who looked like me and whose history I shared in important ways.

The question was something I wrestled with. Did I identify more with my black fellows now that I'd shared the injustices they faced every day? I did, of course. My eyes had been opened. I could never close them to what I learned and what I felt in the South, shoulder to shoulder with my people. That much was undeniable. What was less easy to answer was exactly who *my people* were. Did feeling more black make me feel less Canadian? Did the experience of the Baptist service make me less Anglican?

The answer was, opening your eyes shouldn't make you less anything. It makes you *more*. I was a different man afterward, but I certainly wasn't less. Nothing was taken from me; I gained a great deal.

The service lasted an hour. When it was over I shook the minister's hand; he thanked me for coming and asked if I was new in the area. I told him I was just passing through.

After church ended we had an hour to kill. It was hot, and we were thirsty. When we spotted a diner I looked for a sign that said "Whites Only" but couldn't see one. Right inside the front door were four empty seats, so we sat down. There were three or four white guys at the counter who looked at us as if we were some kind of plague that had walked in. They said something to the waiter, who came over and made a crude racial remark.

That was all we needed to hear. We got up and walked out. I stood by the side of the road for forty-two minutes waiting for that bus to bring me back to training camp, thinking only about the bus that would, eventually, get me out of this nightmare.

During training camp we'd learn our assignments in the morning from sheets of colored paper the coaches would put up on the barracks' bulletin boards. The one sheet you didn't want to have your name on was the pink sheet, which said "Will the players listed below please report to the manager's office before nine o'clock this morning." If your name appeared on this list, it meant you were being sent home.

It was in week three when I saw my name on the pink sheet. I was kind of relieved. The manager told me that they were impressed by my play but thought I needed "a little more seasoning." So they were going to send me home. Not by airplane this time, but by bus.

It was a five-day trip. As we moved north I'd get off the bus periodically to use the restroom or grab a sandwich, and when I got back on I'd move a little further up. By the time we reached the Canadian border I was sitting at the front.

And by the time I got home to Fredericton I'd seen my athletic future clearly—and it was not going to be playing baseball in the States. I told myself to forget that game plan, to concentrate on hockey, and that's what I did.

Even so, I'd have to step back onto the ice as a one-eyed hockey player, and that was something I thought about a lot.

I was visiting my sister Thelma one day in early summer when someone knocked on her door. After she'd gone to answer it, I heard her call out to me. "Willie," she said, "there's a Mr. Imlach here to see you."

She sounded a little apprehensive, as if this white man at the door wearing a fedora in summer might be looking for trouble. But no, George "Punch" Imlach was looking for me. In fact, he said he just "happened to be in the neighborhood," even though he was nearly a thousand miles away from his own neighborhood.

Toronto-born Punch Imlach stood about five eight and wasn't a particularly big fellow, but in the world of hockey he was a very big man. He'd go on to become one of the legendary coaches in the National Hockey League, guiding the Toronto Maple Leafs to four Stanley Cup championships. Back on that day in 1956, though, Punch was the coach of the Quebec Aces, a professional team in Quebec City, and he wanted me to be an Ace, too. "Willie, I'm putting together a championship team," he told me, "and you're the kind of player we need."

I was fast, that was for sure, and I was good with the puck. I'd managed to finish my junior season with Kitchener. But the Aces were a big step up to the Quebec Hockey League, which was minor pro. How would my one-eyed-self do on a bigger stage?

Of course, Thelma didn't know about my blind right eye; for years and years no one except my sister Betty ever knew. But since I'd made it through baseball camp without its being an issue, it wasn't going to be an issue now. So I listened as Punch laid out his offer: $3,500 for the year and a $500 signing bonus.

Now, in 1956, $4,000 a year was very good money. But I figured he hadn't come all this way without being willing to give a little more. So I said, "Punch, if you're putting together a championship team, that means we're going to the playoffs. I'd like another $300 if we make the playoffs and another bonus of $300 if I score twenty goals."

It was pretty bold of me, but Punch didn't run out of the room screaming obscenities. I didn't know it at the time, but he did not like to part with money, not even a penny. And yet on this day he thought about it for a moment and then agreed to my terms. He really wanted me on his team.

Now all I had to do was make the Quebec Aces, score twenty goals, and keep my blind eye a secret. Then I would truly have a shot at the NHL. You might think I was crazy, but I believed I could do it. And now I finally had my best chance yet to transform that belief into reality.

6.

ISLAND LAKE

I had a lot to think about in that summer of 1956. And not just about my life in hockey, once summer was over. These were exciting times the world over. Elvis Presley made his first appearance on *The Ed Sullivan Show*, thrilling everyone with his voice, his moves, and this new thing called rock and roll. As it happened, on the day of Presley's debut, Ed Sullivan—who'd been opposed to having Presley on until he learned how he'd boosted a rival's ratings—was in hospital recuperating from a car accident. And Elvis wasn't there either: he performed from a CBS studio in Hollywood, where he was filming his first movie. So substitute host Charles Laughton, the star of *Mutiny on the Bounty* in the year I was born, announced from the New York stage, "Away to Hollywood to meet Elvis Presley!" More than sixty million people heard Elvis sing "Don't Be Cruel,"

"Love Me Tender," "Hound Dog," and a Little Richard song, "Ready Teddy."

It was a wonderful time for sports in Canada as well: the Montreal Canadiens had won their eighth Stanley Cup by defeating the Detroit Red Wings in five games, and William John Potts, the guy with the golden heart and fists of iron, known as "Whipper Billy Watson," was the first Canadian to win the World Heavyweight Wrestling Championship, defeating the American champ, Lou Thesz, in Toronto. Meanwhile, I'd been to the Deep South and survived.

Training camp with the Aces was more than a month away when I made my annual pilgrimage to a place that still provides me with all those benefits you get when you meditate. I went to Island Lake to think about it all.

I'd been going to the lake, which is more than a hundred miles north of Fredericton, with my brother Richard since I was a boy. So in the summer of 1956 I drove up there with Coot, his son Dougie, and my pal Junior Doherty to do what I loved almost as much as I loved hockey: go fishing. The lake, a little bigger than a half square mile, is fed by springs that ripple out from its bed, which is just over forty feet down at its deepest point. And at fifteen hundred feet above sea level, even if it's scorching hot in August, the water is cool. Plus it's set in the pristine New Brunswick wilderness, with its crisp clean air, vast forests, and a lot of trout. In fact, Island Lake is home to New Brunswick brook trout. They're the only species in the lake (aside from the baitfish), and have been so since the Ice Age ended. Fishing there is like fishing history.

When I first started going, the place didn't have the "modern" conveniences it has now: no grocery shops, no hotels, and not even any electricity or plumbing. There was just you, your wits, and the great outdoors. We'd bring camping gear and fishing rods and would set up camp over a weekend or longer in summer. In the summer of 1956, we were there for a week.

Getting to Island Lake was not for the faint of heart. Today you can stay at a resort and just walk out the door, but back then it meant a serious hike through the forest. I remember one time Richard built a lean-to with branches over our tents, a process we called "bowering." There was a storm that night, and Junior and I woke up to see Coot out of his sleeping bag, thrashing around: the bower had failed and he had to repair it as the rain pounded down. To this day we still get a laugh out of that night. When something needs to be fixed, we'll still say, "Better bower that" or "That's going to need some bowering."

At Island Lake I learned how to look after myself in the most basic way. If you didn't catch any fish, you were going to go hungry. If you didn't find fresh water, you were going to be thirsty. And if you didn't bower your camp properly, you were going to be dinner for the insects, not to mention at the mercy of the wind and the rain and the jokes for decades afterward.

The reality of having to rely on your own resources is something that stuck with me. Cub Scouts and Boy Scouts had taught me a few things about how to survive in the wilderness, but out there on Island Lake I learned a different kind of teamwork by looking out for my companions as much as they were looking out for me. We were all in this great adventure, and what was good for one was good for all.

I've noted that I'm competitive, and so I loved the fishing contests we'd have to see who could catch the biggest trout. We'd always throw back the little ones, and I'd always try to win. I usually did, just because I wouldn't give up until I got that big trout hooked. The sun might be setting, but I was determined it would be me who provided the biggest fish for dinner.

At the end of the day we'd build a campfire, then fry up the trout in a bit of butter and roast the potatoes we'd brought. Along with a couple of beers (not for Coot, who never drank or smoked), it would be a regular feast. Then, as night fell, we'd talk about life.

That summer of 1956, I talked to Richard and Junior about my upcoming season as a pro hockey player. They were happy for me, of course, and Richard, who'd never made it to the ranks himself, was proud that I'd made it this far. But out on Island Lake I dared to tell them that I planned to go even further. I just didn't tell them about my eye. I wasn't even tempted: I'd buried that secret so deep within me that I almost forgot about it. Almost.

At night, with a million stars twinkling off into the forever of that black sky, it didn't seem as if there were any limits to what we wanted to do down here on earth, and that we should be aiming higher. The vastness of the heavens also made human cruelties to each other seem even smaller and sadder than they are. But I looked to the positive side of things, imagining what I wanted to do when I got to the Quebec Aces and pulled on their storied jersey.

"You'll be a great one, Willie," Richard said. Junior joked that I'd *better* make the team, given how much he loved going to Quebec City, with its pretty women and fine food, and how he wanted to make the most of both while he could.

Richard and Dougie are both dead now, leaving me and Junior to keep the fishing flame alive. But before Richard died of heart problems he asked me to return to Island Lake one more time for him. I did, and it was emotional. I fished, just as he'd wanted me to. And as the moose, deer, and beaver watched me reel in trout, I felt at peace. Island Lake puts life in perspective.

Looking back on that summer now, it seems, like so many things do, as if it was just yesterday, although don't ask me what I had for breakfast because I might not remember that. In my mind's eye I can still see me and Richard and Dougie and Junior, sitting around the campfire, the trout on the fry pan. We're laughing about some joke, all of life before us. And the best days of my hockey life just around the corner.

7.

THE QUEBEC ACES

When we think of professional hockey today, the NHL rightly pops into mind first. It did when I was just starting out as well. But in those days we had lots of professional opportunities, and in the interest of job security, many players would choose to stay in a "minor" professional league. After all, you could remain there for the rest of your playing days, into your thirties and beyond, and earn about $4,000 a year. Or you could risk everything in the NHL, which, at the time, had only six teams, with each team dressing about twenty-two players, give or take. So you could say that, in total, there were 132 or so jobs in the NHL. Compare that to the five minor pro leagues, and you can see where a player had a better chance of catching on and staying put.

Still, if you shone in the minor pro leagues, the NHL might notice. It was just a matter of getting a pro contract. And so when I got my shot with the Quebec Aces, I considered myself the luckiest man in hockey.

The Aces played in the Quebec Hockey League, a postwar creation that had teams across the province (as well as the Hull-Ottawa Junior Canadiens). "Aces" sounds like a great name for a team, but it was actually an acronym (with some shifting around of vowels) for the firm that owned it—the Anglo-Canadian Pulp and Paper Company. In French, the team was known as Les As.

And the Aces, although a fairly recent team, were rich in history. Three seasons before I pulled on their green, red, and white jersey with the four ace cards in the middle of its crest, Jean Béliveau himself played for the As. As a center he was without equal, stickhandling the puck as if his brain were connected directly to it, then dishing it off to teammates right in the middle of their tape. He was also your classic tall, dark, and handsome guy, and the women loved him. Actually, everybody loved Béliveau. Quebec City businesses showered him with suits and hats and shirts and free steak lunches every time he scored three goals.

The Aces gave Béliveau a contract for $20,000 a year, along with two cars. One of them was a stylish convertible with the license plate "2B." Given that the premier of Quebec, the powerful conservative Maurice Duplessis, had the license plate "1B," it would be like giving an NHL superstar his own private jet and calling it Air Force Two. And Béliveau wasn't even in the NHL yet.

The Montreal Canadiens owned his NHL rights and very much wanted him to suit up for them, a chance that any of us would have jumped at. Béliveau, however, was happy in Quebec City. He kept saying no—he was going to keep playing for the Aces and enjoy life. He, too, knew that life in the minor pros was much more secure than in the NHL, and at age twenty-two, he was making a fortune.

In desperation, the Canadiens finally did something that would be extraordinary in any era: they bought the entire Quebec Senior Hockey League. So now they owned the Aces, and they owned Jean Béliveau. But Béliveau, who always took the high road, decided this was a signal that the time had come to play in the NHL. And so, before any kind of ugly battle could become public, he signed with the Canadiens.

There was actually another guy who'd played for the Aces who was just as great. But he never made it to the NHL for a very different reason, one directly connected to me.

Herb Carnegie had grown up in Toronto and played pond hockey there. In the 1940s he made his name playing for Sherbrooke, another Quebec League team. Herbie was black, and played on an all-black line with his brother Ossie and Manny McIntyre. Like Béliveau, he was a magician with the puck and a creative, beautiful player. His passes to his brother and to McIntyre were what we called "lamp lighters." After you got one, in full flight, right on your tape, all you had to do was tap the puck into the net and light the goal lamp. Playing alongside Herbie made good players better.

Herb Carnegie won three Most Valuable Player awards when he played with Sherbrooke, plus a championship trophy.

In the early 1950s he was playing on the Quebec Aces with Jean Béliveau, who thought the world of him. It made the hair on my neck stand up to sit in the same dressing room those giants had sat in.

But the difference between these two giants is that the white one made the NHL and the black one didn't. How could a guy who'd won not one but three MVP awards not be in the NHL?

Carnegie's Jamaican-born father had warned him of this when he was a kid, telling him, "They won't let any black boys in the National Hockey League." Years later, those terrible words would ring true. In 1938, while playing for the Toronto Junior Rangers under coach Ed Wildey, the eighteen-year-old Carnegie began attracting NHL attention. His junior team was practicing in Maple Leaf Gardens, home to the Toronto Maple Leafs, when he was spotted by Conn Smythe—an epic, eccentric character. Smythe had had success as an athlete, had fought in the First World War, and had gambled a small fortune to create the Leafs. He was a vocal and public patriot: hence the name of his team, derived from the badges Canadian soldiers wore on their uniforms.

Smythe was also a bigot. He pretty much didn't trust anyone who wasn't white and Protestant. In fact, his Leafs, like Toronto itself at the time, were segregated—not along black–white lines, but Catholic–Protestant. Catholic prospects went to the "dogan" school, which is what he called St. Michael's College School. He wanted to keep them from polluting the Protestant kids on the Leafs for as long as he could.

It was Carnegie's coach, Ed Wildey, who told him that Smythe had seen how talented a player he was and said he'd sign him for the Leafs the next day, but for one thing: "I'll give any man $10,000 who can turn Herb Carnegie white."

It was a cruel, terrible thing to say to a kid, especially one who'd grown up idolizing the Toronto Maple Leafs. It haunted Herb Carnegie for the rest of his long life.

There is some doubt today whether Smythe actually said those words—whether Wildey had just given voice to the prejudice of the team—but Smythe did see Carnegie play, and he knew how good he was. He could have signed him for the Leafs. So he kept him out of the NHL, if not by word then by deed, or lack thereof, one that rippled throughout the league because Conn Smythe was a powerful man in that kingdom. Professional hockey could have beaten baseball at breaking the color barrier if the Leafs had signed Carnegie, but they didn't.

Things looked like they might change in 1948. Herb Carnegie finally got his shot at the NHL when he was invited to the New York Rangers' training camp. Even though Carnegie was as good as—if not better than—the best players, the Rangers still wanted him to spend a season on one of their farm teams. This is what the Brooklyn Dodgers had done with Jackie Robinson.

The Rangers would give Carnegie $2,700 to play for their lowest-level minor league team in Tacoma, Washington. Carnegie was already making $5,100 playing for Sherbrooke and supplementing that with outside work in Quebec, so he said no thanks. The next day the Rangers increased their offer to $4,700 and a place on their St. Paul United States Hockey League team, which was a higher league, but Carnegie again said no. Finally, after a week of training camp, the Rangers upped the placement to the New Haven Ramblers, their top farm team. But Carnegie had a wife and three children to support, and he couldn't afford to say yes.

So while some people have said it was Herb Carnegie who turned down the NHL, you have to look at it from his point of view. He'd get to play on a farm team for less money than he was making in Quebec and with no guarantee that he'd ever make the NHL. And maybe the Rangers would have brought Carnegie to the NHL in a year or so, or maybe they wouldn't have. They certainly didn't call him up when four of their players were injured in a car crash just before that season started, including their two top centers, Buddy O'Connor and Edgar Laprade. But Carnegie never got a call from the Rangers again. I think that tells us all we need to know.

One person of color who did play for the Rangers, for one shift in one game, was Chinese Canadian Larry Kwong. On March 13, 1948, at the Montreal Forum, Kwong made his NHL debut with the Blueshirts, wearing number 11, against the Montreal Canadiens. Kwong had to watch from the bench until late in the third period before seeing the ice for his only shift of the night. Playing for only about a minute, he tallied no points in what would be his only big league game.

Kwong was the top scorer on the New York Rovers, a Rangers farm team in the Quebec Senior Hockey League. Yet Kwong watched as less productive white players got called up to the NHL team. Figuring he never would get that magical phone call, Kwong, too, did the smart thing and in the off-season accepted a more lucrative offer to play for the rival Valleyfield Braves, also of the Quebec League.

You can say, then, that Larry Kwong was the first player to break the color barrier, and that I was the first black player. And yet people see me more as the pioneer—because of racism against black people in pro sport at the time, because my career in the NHL was longer, and because I echoed Jackie Robinson's triumph in being the first black player to crack the premier league. Let's just say that what Herb Carnegie and Larry Kwong experienced didn't go away when I made the NHL.

In my first season with Quebec, although Carnegie and Béliveau were gone from the Aces, their presence could still be felt in the locker room. It was Béliveau who'd said that the young players learn from the older ones, and we were learning from the stories of legends. I was going to do everything I could to live up to the level of excellence they had established.

Meanwhile, I would enjoy the city. I'd played there as a junior with the Frontenacs, and I loved the place. At the time it had about a quarter of a million people, and its long, cold, snowy winters were great for hockey. Also, I had no problem going into any of the great restaurants in "Vieux-Quebec," the old town, and ordering whatever I wanted in French. Not only had I lived in the city before, but I'd lived with both English and French in Fredericton. I could talk to the fans and read what the papers said about us. Some athletes

avoid this at all costs, but I found the sports coverage enter-
taining, since the reports were sometimes so far from what I'd
seen on the ice—in the game in which I'd actually played—
that it seemed as if I were reading fiction. Still, in Quebec
they knew their hockey, so the sports pages in the province's
papers were pretty accurate and very opinionated.

I even took a business course in French at O'Sullivan
Business College. I've always wished I'd learned more lan-
guages. Today I can still get by in French, although I can
write it much better than I speak it. And since I live in San
Diego, I know a bit of Spanish, too.

So I was very happy to roll back into Quebec for training
camp in September of 1956. I was also as nervous as I could
be. Not only was this my first time in the pros; it was also the
first time I'd be playing with only one good eye.

The first thing I had to do was pass the physical, which
was nothing like pro sport physicals today. NHL teams now
test everything about a player, including his mind and his
social media profile. But in my day we went into the training
room, and there was a doctor with a nurse. We'd get weighed
and have our reflexes tested. They'd check our breathing and
our heart rate, and ask if we had any other issues we wanted
to bring up. I said nothing, figuring that, "Yes, I think you
should know I'm blind in my right eye" wouldn't be a winning play to make. I was just grateful that no one thought
to give us an eye test—not then or at any other time in my
twenty-one-year professional career.

———

My first training camp with the Aces gave me a taste of what the championship season was going to be like. Punch Imlach was huge as a coach. Like almost all hockey coaches, he'd been a player, meaning he came to coaching from the inside, as it were. He played some of his early hockey in Toronto's Bank Leagues (teams sponsored by banks and companies), and then moved up to the senior leagues. It was while he was playing for the Toronto Goodyears in a game in Windsor, Ontario, that he got his nickname.

At one point he was tripped, and when he fell and whacked his head on the ice, he was knocked out cold. The Goodyears' trainer skidded out onto the ice to try to revive the fallen Imlach with smelling salts. Now, Punch was a shifty center-man with a fierce temper that could roar to life at anything, really. So when he regained consciousness, he was furious at having been tripped and threw a punch at the first guy he saw—who happened to be the trainer of his own team.

Some sportswriter in Toronto wrote that Imlach, who was likely concussed, was "punch drunk," a term from boxing that's more serious than it sounds. It describes the unsteadiness that comes from taking too many blows to the head, which is a very real problem these days in all contact sports. The writer kept calling him Punchy Imlach. Then it just got shortened to Punch, and it stuck.

Imlach had played for the Aces himself, and was a pretty good centerman, notching twenty-six goals in his final season, 1948–49, while he was also coaching the team.

His first coaching job was with the Cornwall Flyers, a Second World War army hockey team. After a number of players had died in combat during the First World War, the league had changed its patriotism policy so that players drafted into the armed forces would wind up playing hockey on a military team rather than actually fighting. There weren't going to be any more headlines about yet another star hockey player who died young in battle.

There were, however, exceptions to this: Conn Smythe, owner of the Toronto Maple Leafs, took a Sportsman's Battery off to war—and although no NHL regulars were killed, Smythe himself was nearly finished off during a Luftwaffe bombing raid. Still, it was much safer to be playing hockey in the army than fighting the Nazis.

When the war ended, Imlach had survived, but at a cost. He was twenty-seven years old, which, then and now, was a little long in the tooth to be trying for your first shot at the NHL. Even so, when Imlach was discharged in 1945, he got a tryout with the Detroit Red Wings—and arrived at training camp at the same time as a seventeen-year-old prospect named Gordie Howe. Imlach had also just married, and saw reality staring him in the face: a family to support, and "Mr. Hockey" ahead of him on the depth chart. So he went back to Quebec City and got an accountant's job, as well as a job playing for the Aces.

But in his years playing and coaching for the Aces, the championship trophy had eluded him. Punch also had his sights on the NHL, so he wanted to build a team that would give him—and us—our best shot at the top rung on the professional ladder. In fact, thirteen of the players on the Aces in that 1956–57 season had, or would have, NHL experience.

And we all wanted to go there for the first time—or go back there for a reprise—Punch included.

I learned a lot from him in Quebec, but it was at my first Aces training camp that I learned that if a player didn't have a strong work ethic, there was no room for him on Imlach's Quebec Aces. So I worked twice as hard as I ever had. In drills I could cheat a bit, moving in a way that I could see the puck, but when we had scrimmages and I played on left wing, I had to rely on my speed to keep me from being stapled to the boards by a bodycheck I didn't see coming. Meanwhile, off the ice, I ran and lifted weights, doing everything I could to show Imlach that the $4,000 he was paying me (he'd become part owner of the Aces) was not going to be wasted.

I got a nice, inexpensive apartment in Quebec City and made that money go far. In fact, I'd send a bit home to my parents each payday. Hockey actually changed their lives: Harry and Rosebud had been renting on Charlotte Street, but now, thanks to hockey, they could own a place, and so they did.

The mother of the other black family in town, Mrs. Isabell Lawrence, was great friends with my mom. My mother had always loved her house, and one day, after her boys had moved away, Mrs. Lawrence told my mom that it was up for sale. There was money in the bank to buy the house, so I said to my parents, "Go get a real estate agent and let's do it."

Mrs. Lawrence must have felt her life was coming to a close, because by the time we moved in, she was dead. I don't know why she didn't leave the house to her sons. But she just loved my mother, Rosebud, who used to cook for her, and I used to shovel her driveway and clean snow off her steps, so maybe she just wanted us to have a home of our own.

Once we'd moved in we fixed up the house, which was smaller than the one we'd been living in across the street. But there was a cellar downstairs, dark and cool, where my mom could can and store our vegetables. It was such a relief to my parents to know they were in their own place and that it was all paid for.

That's one of the things I was proudest of: hockey had given me money to help them buy a house. They'd always made a home for me, a wonderful place I'd go back to in a second if I could time travel. And now I was able to help make a home for them. It makes me proud still.

So did playing for Punch Imlach. He's earned a reputation as being a hard guy to get along with, but I think he was the fairest coach I ever played for. He had a simple philosophy, which he would tell us all the time: "Play hard, dress like a pro, and have money in your pocket."

He swore a lot, and he was very superstitious, especially when it came to buying new hats and suits before games. Some have even said that he was mean, but I can't say enough good things about Punch. He'd stand at center ice, whistle in hand, and yell at us to work harder, to go after that puck. "I want you guys to get mad!" he'd shout, and we *would* get mad—at the puck, at each other, and sometimes at him.

Punch was the type of guy who liked a fast, aggressive hockey player, and that was me. If you worked hard, played both ends of the ice, and went full-out after the puck, he was the easiest coach in the world. If you didn't, then in all likelihood you wouldn't be playing on his team for very long.

That's what made him a champion. He wanted to win, and sure enough, in my first pro season, the team finished in first place with eighty-seven points—thirteen points better than the second-place team, Chicoutimi. I myself had a good year, scoring twenty-two goals and adding twelve assists, so I got that $300 bonus. And since we made the playoffs, that other $300 kicked in as well. In the final series we beat the Brandon Manitoba Regals and won the championship for all the minor pro leagues: the Duke of Edinburgh's Trophy. We were the best team in the country in a league that wasn't the NHL.

It was during that first year of pro hockey, though, that I realized getting to the NHL wouldn't be any easier than getting to the Quebec Aces. In many ways, it was harder. I was starting to see how racism had stacked the cards against me. And no matter how much I let it roll off my back, sometimes I just couldn't.

I heard my first racial insult at twelve, when two brothers at school used the N-word on me. At that age kids start to see the world with a harsher eye, and they can take on the worst traits of adults without realizing the damage they're causing. Puzzled by such a sudden, unprovoked attack, I told Coot about it. He had a word with the brothers, and they never bothered me again. I wish I could say the same about adult fans in the province of Quebec, who treated me worse than in anyplace I've ever played.

Now, the fans in Quebec *City* were great, but I was a twenty-plus goal scorer on the home team. There was another black player on the roster, Stan Maxwell; we'd joined the Aces in the same season. Not only was he was from Truro, Nova Scotia, and so a Maritimer like me; he also came from a big family, with even more kids than my own. Stan got his first pair of skates at a rummage sale, he told me, and scored his first five hundred goals between rocks on a frozen pond. That early training must have paid off: Stan was a silky centerman who could put a pass right on your tape in a hundred different ways. And outside of my brother Richard, Stan was my best buddy in hockey. As the only two black guys playing in the Quebec League, we were treated very well in Quebec City, as if we were princes in exile in this wonderful old hockey-mad town. The problems, for me and Stan, happened when we went on road trips, and the worst place of all was Chicoutimi.

Chicoutimi is a town about a hundred miles north of Quebec City, on the Saguenay River; its local team was called the Saguenéens. The place was almost entirely francophone, and had been for a very long time, so pretty much everyone who came into town was an "outsider." And if you were black, well, you might as well have come from the moon.

As soon as I stepped onto the ice in the Chicoutimi barn I could hear the chants and the name-calling. *"Maudit negre"* was the most common one, which means something like "damned Negro."

Sometimes I'd get a penalty for something or other, and off I'd go to the penalty box. In my first season with the Aces I racked up eighty minutes in penalties (my highest total until 1974, when I notched eighty-nine minutes in the sin bin). In those days there was no glass between the fans and the player sitting in the penalty box, so if someone wanted to, they could come right down from the stands and have a conversation with you face to face, as it were.

So there I was, sitting in the Chicoutimi penalty box. I'd just taken off my gloves to grab a drink of water when I heard the crowd chanting the usual unimaginative *"maudit negre"* refrain. But when the chanting got louder, I suspected they were cheering someone on—and that the someone was coming up behind me in the penalty box. Needless to say, the guy wasn't likely coming by to say hello.

I didn't turn around. I just waited, listening for the sound of a shoe stepping onto the floor of the penalty box. When I heard it, I turned fast (to my left, of course) and saw the guy who was about to jump me. I met him with one clean punch. He went flying backwards.

This did not make the Chicoutimi fans happy. Now they were screaming for blood, and some of them started to climb down toward me in the penalty box. But my teammates came to the rescue, and soon we had a real brawl, with guys duking it out all over the ice and my teammates trying to get me out of the box.

The guy who'd planned to attack me got up with a bloody nose, and although he tried to escape back up the stairs, he was blocked by screaming fans. I could have landed a couple more punches on him, but I'd made my point.

It was ugly, and it certainly wasn't isolated.

Sometimes people would spit on me or throw drinks on me. My parents had always said that life in hockey would be difficult and that the world was filled with racists. I certainly knew that to be true during my time playing in Quebec, and I would know it again, but I wasn't going to quit.

I told myself I'd quit only if my skills slowed down to the point where I couldn't compete. I wasn't about to let a bunch of stupid, ignorant people chase me out of pro hockey. I was going to show everyone that I could play with the best.

And I was just getting started.

8.

CAMP BIG LEAGUE

In the summer of 1957 I was feeling great, all things considered. I'd just come off my first professional hockey season, having scored more than twenty goals and with my name on a championship trophy. And I could still hear the words Phil Watson, my Quebec Frontenacs junior coach, had said: that if I applied myself, I had the skills to make the NHL. All I cared about was proving him right about my skills. But the world's greatest hockey league was tough to get into, no matter what color you were.

The period between 1942 and 1967 has come down to us as the golden age of the NHL's Original Six, but it wasn't original, and it certainly wasn't golden. The six teams that formed this mythic union were the Boston Bruins, Toronto Maple Leafs, Montreal Canadiens, Chicago Black Hawks, Detroit

Red Wings, and New York Rangers. In 1917, when the NHL was formed, the only one of these that actually existed was Montreal. And in 1942, when the NHL's New York/Brooklyn Americans folded, it was the Canadiens, along with the other five, that were the surviving clubs. Those six teams would make up the NHL until the league doubled in size in 1967.

But back in 1957 there were thirty-two teams in the minor pro leagues, each carrying twenty-three guys. So if you add those 736 minor league guys to the 132 or so in the NHL, there were roughly 862 guys already playing hockey at a high level who were after those 132 NHL jobs. That meant you had a one in six shot at making the NHL. But it was actually tougher than that, because guys like Jean Béliveau and Gordie Howe and Terry Sawchuk and Jacques Plante and Andy Bathgate and Bronco Horvath and a whole bunch of other stars were permanent NHL fixtures and not part of the equation. Their spots were taken. There weren't really 132 spots available.

And the NHL was about to undergo a major business transformation. Hockey players, like baseball players, were trying to form a union. A few months earlier, in February 1957, Doug Harvey of Montreal and Ted Lindsay, captain of Detroit, had spearheaded the formation of the National Hockey League Players' Association. The NHLPA sued the league over several issues: provision of player pensions, payment of salaries during training camp, meal allowances on the road, and payment for playing exhibition games. They also wanted to establish a "no trade" clause after a guy had spent six years in the league with a specific team.

It was a bold initiative, one that would eventually change the nature of professional sports. At the time, though, the league and the owners saw it as treason. And as a real threat to their power.

As a result, Ted Lindsay of Detroit was stripped of his captaincy. Then, most shocking of all, on July 23, 1957, while hockey writers were at the beach, Lindsay—one of the toughest, best players in the NHL—was traded to the lowly Chicago Black Hawks. The message was clear: no one was untouchable if he crossed the NHL's powers that be.

I wasn't looking for trouble, and to be honest, I was looking at the NHL's labor stuff as a twenty-one-year-old guy trying to raise the level of his game. I knew guys wanted to hold on to whatever job they had, and sure, I'd made more money than ever before that past season in Quebec City. I wasn't looking to lose my job. I was looking to get a better one.

Back in those days, professional athletes—even NHL players— had to hold down jobs in the summer to make ends meet. So in the summer of 1957 I was back home working in a service station, pumping gas and changing oil and checking tire pressure and so on. I liked the job, as I liked meeting people. I knew a lot of them, and they knew me too as a hockey player, so I had fun talking about the game with my customers.

Coot was driving a three-ton truck for a produce company called Willett Food, delivering fruits and vegetables to small country stores. Sometimes I'd go with him on his rounds and he'd let me drive the truck along the dirt roads. So I learned to drive on this massive beast with a stick shift, but since I didn't know any differently it was fine with me.

One August day I came home from the service station and my mother told me I had mail. The way she said it, though, with a hopeful smile and a twinkle in her eye, wasn't because I was her favorite baby boy. She knew the letter was something I wanted.

So I picked up my letter and looked at the return address. It was postmarked from Boston. Better still, it was from the Boston Bruins. I felt my chest swell as I slowly opened the envelope, not wanting to jinx what I hoped was inside: my ticket to the NHL.

Now, the Boston Bruins didn't have as deep a system of farm teams as other clubs did. Whereas the Montreal Canadiens, say, or Toronto Maple Leafs had layers of talent spread across several leagues, the Bruins had working agreements with professional teams like the Quebec Aces. This meant that Boston could invite players in the minor pro leagues to try out for them, and even have them sent up to fill a gap on the NHL squad.

The letter was from the team's general manager, Lynn Patrick, who came from one of pro hockey's pioneer families. In fact, to call them pioneers understates their influence on the game, which pretty much turned it into the game we love today. Back in 1912 Lynn's dad, Lester, and his uncle, Frank, started a professional hockey league out on Canada's West Coast, with teams in Vancouver, Victoria, and New Westminster. They built the biggest rink in the world: Vancouver's Denman Arena could seat 10,500 hockey fans, 2,500 more than Madison Square Garden in New York. And since you don't get much ice or snow out in the West Coast, the Patricks installed artificial ice in their arenas to make sure their teams could play when Mother Nature wasn't cooperating.

They soon had teams in Seattle, Washington, and Portland, Oregon. If you ever want to win a bar bet, ask someone who thinks they know hockey to name the first American team to win the Stanley Cup. If they're pretty knowledgeable, they'll say the New York Rangers in 1928, but they'd be wrong. It was the Seattle Metropolitans in 1917. They played in the Patricks' league back when the Stanley Cup was a challenge trophy, meaning that teams finishing at the top of a recognized league could challenge the current holder of the Cup to play for it. In the early days of hockey there could be two or three challenges in a season, and in 1917 the Metropolitans of the Patricks' Pacific Coast Hockey Association defeated the Montreal Canadiens of the National Hockey Association three games to one. (That's the double-or-nothing bet, just in case they get the Metropolitans right in the first wager.)

I had a great fondness for the Patricks, responsible as they were for creating the game I was now playing, although I didn't realize how much until years later when I started to learn more hockey history. (They don't teach you that when you learn to skate.) For instance, the Patricks invented the blue line. In early hockey, you couldn't pass the puck forward. You could only pass it sideways, the way they pass the ball in rugby. But with the invention of the blue line players could pass the puck forward between each team's blue line—which made the game faster and more creative and more exciting.

The Patricks also invented line changes, the penalty shot, the farm team system, the playoff system, the power play, the ability of goalies to fall in making saves (before they had to stand upright, though there's also evidence that the Maritimes' Coloured League was first on this front), numbers on jerseys, and a few other things. Really, they pretty much invented the modern game.

Lynn Patrick himself had played ten seasons for the New York Rangers at center and left wing and had won a Stanley Cup. So you could say that getting anything from Lynn Patrick was a big deal, even if he started his letter to me in a way that made me smile.

"Dear Bill," it began—no one but strangers called me Bill.

The Boston Bruins will hold their training camp here in Boston at the Boston Garden. We will begin our train-ing period on the afternoon of Sunday, September 15. We would like you to report to the Manger Hotel in Boston before noon on September 15.

I felt a wave of emotion flood over me. I was going to get my shot at the NHL—if I made it out of the Bruins train-ing camp. But that didn't matter then, because a door had opened, a very big door, to a place where I'd promised myself I'd go when I was just fourteen years old.

Then my mother brought me back to earth by asking me how many black players were in the NHL. It was one of those questions to which she already knew the answer, but that was the point.

"There's none," I told her. "I could be the first."

She thought about this, and then very gently said, "We hope it happens, but you've got to think of the worst."

That was just like them, worrying that Lynn Patrick had sent the letter to the wrong guy—that there'd been a mistake, that they wanted the white Willie O'Ree, not the black one. But I knew there was no mistake: there was only one Willie O'Ree, and he was going to the Bruins training camp. I framed that letter and I have it still.

Even though I'd been dreaming of the NHL for years, in that summer of 1957 I was thinking of the two-year contract I'd signed to play with the Quebec Aces. This invitation from the Bruins was unexpected, and while hugely welcome, I wondered how I was going to explain my good fortune to Stan Maxwell without making him feel forgotten, and how I would explain it to Punch.

But when I called Stan to tell him my news, he had some of his own: he'd received a letter from Lynn Patrick as well. We were both going to the Bruins training camp, and with Punch's blessing. The wily coach knew that if the Bruins were asking for two of his players, the NHL had their eyes on him as well.

———

So Stan and I took the train down to Boston. I'd never been before, but I'd heard things: that it was home to some of the country's finest universities and was known for its progressive politics. It was also known for being a nakedly racist city.

And yet, back in 1950, it was the Boston Celtics owner, Walter Brown, who'd drafted Chuck Cooper, the NBA's first black player. But a year later, in 1951, it was also Brown who refused to let Korean runners enter the famous Boston Marathon. At the time the United States was at war in Korea, joining forces with the south against the communist north. "While American soldiers are fighting and dying in Korea," Brown said, "every Korean should be fighting to protect his country instead of training for marathons." He made no comment on why American runners were entering the marathon that year when other Americans were off fighting the communists. In this Brown seemed to represent Boston's strange contradictions: progressive on the one hand, but highly, shall we say, conservative on the other.

Which is to say that I went into Boston prepared for anything. At least it wasn't the Deep South, where racism underpinned the structure of society and the ghosts of slavery were everywhere.

I immediately liked the city. It had been the active center before, during, and after the American War of Independence, so it was rich in history. And with its brick buildings and green public spaces, it also had a European feel to it. I hadn't yet been to Europe, but I'd seen photographs and films of its great cities, and Boston reminded me of them. I thought I could be happy playing here.

But first I had to get through training camp. Although I'd managed to keep my blindness hidden from the Quebec Aces, now I was taking a major step up to the best league in the world. Could I pull it off?

For Stan and me, just stepping onto the ice at Boston Garden was like making the NHL. There we were, two black guys, skating for our lives to join one of the league's great teams. And to see its pedigree, all we had to do was look up: for there on the Garden's rafters hung the three Stanley Cup banners from 1929, 1939, and 1941. Would the 1957–58 season bring another? Would my name be etched on that Cup?

At the time, though, I was thinking more about the current Bruins lineup than the glory teams of yesteryear or what might happen come the playoffs. Some NHL teams had one training camp for rookies and another for veteran players, but not Boston. We were all there together, new guys like me and established stars like Doug Mohns, Don McKenney (the nicest guy I ever played with, always giving me encouragement), Fleming Mackell, Fern Flaman, Allan Stanley, Leo Boivin, Vic Stasiuk, Johnny Bucyk, and Jerry Toppazzini. Stanley, Boivin, Flaman, and Bucyk would all make it to the Hockey Hall of Fame. It was that kind of team.

The veteran Bruins treated Stan and me as if we belonged. That was such a bonus, since it meant we could relax and play our best game. Now, at some NHL training camps, rookies are seen as a target. They're younger than the veterans and thought to be after their jobs, so the older guys will do everything they can to make their life difficult. But it wasn't like that in Boston in 1957. We were like brothers.

They'd booked the entire team at the same hotel, the Hotel Manger. I'd never seen so much marble in my life. It was first class, and just staying there made me feel as if I were already a full-fledged member of the Bruins. Of course, Milt Schmidt, the Bruins coach, had us living at that grand old hotel for another reason: to start team bonding right out of the gate. And he moved in himself so that he could prowl the halls to enforce our eleven p.m. curfew.

We all had to be up by seven a.m. and we all had to show up for breakfast, too: necessary fuel for the demanding practices Schmidt ran. The Bruins weren't loaded with superstars—at least, guys who were superstars yet, though Johnny Bucyk would sure become one—so hard work was the order of the day. I was fine with that. It had always been my order of the day, every day.

Bucyk, whose heritage was Ukrainian, was nicknamed the "Chief" because a Boston cartoonist thought he looked Native American. He and Vic Stasiuk and Bronco Horvath formed Boston's "Uke Line," back in the day when it was acceptable to identify players by their ethnicity. (In the 1970s, the New York Rangers even had the "Mafia Line": Phil Esposito, who is of Italian ancestry and whom they called the Godfather, along with Don Maloney and Don Murdoch. The Godfather and two Dons.) And of course, Schmidt himself, once a league-leading scorer, had been part of the most famous "ethnic" line of all time: the Bruins' "Kraut Line," so named because all three forwards were German Canadians. This was right before the Second World War. The three "Krauts" would soon join the Royal Canadian Air Force and ship out to fight the Nazis, but not before Boston fans carried them off the ice on their shoulders after their final game. (They all returned, and Schmidt resumed his All Star-level play when the war was over.)

He was also an All-Star coach. If you played for a Milt Schmidt Bruins team in the late 1950s, you knew that what you lacked in firepower, you'd make up for in conditioning. When we weren't practicing on the ice, we were working out twice a day in the gym.

Today, NHL teams have state-of-the-art weight-training rooms. In addition to the weights themselves, these rooms feature strength-testing machines, elliptical trainers, and stationary bikes that you can program as if you're riding up and down the Rocky Mountains. They have sound systems playing whatever music you want. They have TVs so that you can watch any game anywhere. They have hot tubs and cold tubs and they even have oxygen chambers to speed up the healing of injuries. In fact, some of their injury rooms are so well stocked they'd make hospitals jealous. And today guys work out even after games, with a set list of exercises designed to maintain conditioning and strength throughout the NHL's grueling eighty-two-game season (and maybe another twenty-eight games, if you were to play the four seven-game playoff series to get the sixteen wins you need to get your name etched on the Stanley Cup).

Back in 1957, though, let's just say the concept of the weight room was simpler. There was a set of scales, a couple of whirlpool tubs that looked like giant bathtubs, a couple of stationary bikes, and a table for you to lie on when you got a rubdown. Training for us back then was made up of a lot of skating and a lot of calisthenics. We'd do sit-ups and push-ups on the ice. Our conditioning came only from skating and those exercises. So at the Bruins camp I just had to work on getting my lungs used to the strain of skating fast and hard for short periods of time. It's true—players are that much faster in the NHL, and although I was pretty fast myself, now I was skating with guys who could keep up.

We also played exhibition games—and as a result, the United Press actually noticed that Stan and I were making history. That September a short item appeared in the papers headlined "Two Negroes Play for Bruins Tonight," about a game against Springfield. The report identifies me and Stan Maxwell as the "Negroes," and points out that a Swede would also be part of this exotic debut—the Swede being Sven "Tumba" Johansson, a centerman who wound up playing five games with us as a Quebec Ace in the 1957–58 season.

Camp lasted a couple of weeks, and at the end of it I was so hoping that Milt Schmidt and Lynn Patrick would say, "Willie O'Ree, you're the missing link that will lead Boston to the Stanley Cup championship." Instead, Schmidt and Patrick told both me and Stan that we needed "more seasoning." That makes players sound like steaks, but it's sports talk for returning to the league below and getting a few more knocks or a bit more maturity.

I was disappointed. I felt I'd shown the Bruins what I could do, and that my blind eye hadn't been an issue at all. Stan had been outstanding as well. So we felt confident that, if we returned to the minor pro league and worked hard, we might just get the chance to come back. After all, coaches have always used the minors as a motivator. A guy who's played a few games on the farm is going to be hungrier than a guy who's made the big team straight out of camp. And a hungrier player is a better player. Now that I'd had a taste of the NHL, I knew I wanted to consume the entire meal.

9.

THE CALL, PART 1

My second season with the Quebec Aces began with a coaching change: Punch Imlach, riding our championship win in 1956–57, had moved on to the Springfield Indians in the American Hockey League. It was a big step up from the QHL, since the AHL was pretty much the most direct feeder to the NHL.

So out went the bald, profane, tumultuous guy that was Punch and in came Joe Crozier. Well, Joe was already there, as a defenseman for the Aces; I'd played with him the year before. In the 1957–58 season he also took on the "playing coach" role, which meant he was coaching us as he was also taking regular shifts on defense. (That can't happen these days—the NHL's collective bargaining agreement prohibits it—but back then it wasn't unusual.)

I liked Joe, who'd come up the tough way from Winnipeg: poor and scrambling. He was a broad, six-foot-tall defenseman, smart and hardworking and just six years older than me. But we gave Joe our full attention. He was a good coach who understood the game in a way that he was able to explain to us—which is not a talent many players possess. In fact, I've found that the more talent you have on the ice, the less you have behind the bench. Players who've had to work at the game instead of being blessed with a raft of natural talents have also had to work at understanding how to maximize their potential, and that labor translates into knowledge they can share.

I started the season off strongly, still dreaming of getting back to Boston as soon as I could. When the call-up came, though, it was to Springfield, Massachusetts, where Punch was coaching. Eddie Shore—the fierce, legendary Boston Bruins defenseman, now owner and manager of the Springfield Indians—said he needed me as an emergency player, I'm sure on Punch's recommendation. Even though it's always disruptive to leave your team, being told that you're riding to the rescue in an emergency is always a nice thing to hear.

So off I went to save the day in the American Hockey League. I'd last for six games. But the records don't tell the whole story about that, nor about Eddie Shore.

Playing in Springfield was like being sent to hockey hell. And not because this Massachusetts town was a bad place, but rather because Eddie Shore was such a highly eccentric, curmudgeonly cur that you wondered what had happened in his childhood to make him that way. Was he dropped on his head one time too many? Did his mother not love him? Was he, in fact, a visitor from another planet pretending—and not very well—to be a human being?

For all his faults off the ice, he'd certainly been a champion on it. (He'd remind us of this whenever he thought we were slacking, which was pretty much all the time. "I won my first Stanley Cup before you were a gleam in your daddy's eye," he'd say. As if this was supposed to give him special insight into hockey, or into our fathers, for that matter.) Eddie had been good at sports as a kid in Cupar, Saskatchewan, a tiny place of about five hundred people just northeast of Regina. Actually, though, he started playing hockey only after being bullied into it by his older brother, who thought his relative lack of interest in the game made him some kind of alien. His teasing got to the point that, at the relatively old age of eighteen, Eddie flicked a switch in his head and went to work. Which may explain part of what made him tick.

For there was one thing that Eddie and I had in common: we'd compete with anything to win. In fact, Eddie got serious about hockey in a way that makes me look as if I were taking every other day off. He'd practice on frozen ponds when it was forty below with wind so fierce his nose, cheeks, and feet would freeze and frost would form on his shoulders. Nothing could stop Eddie from proving his brother wrong, although, in the end, he proved his brother right.

Eddie Shore was one good hockey player. But he'd played the game very much his own way: he wanted to win every second that he was on the ice. Here's an example: back in 1924, when at the age of twenty-two he was playing for the Melville (Saskatchewan) Millionaires in a championship match against the Winnipeg Monarchs, Shore's coach told him to stay out of the penalty box—just to give his team a fighting chance to win without actually fighting. For as bad as it would be to play for Shore years later, it was a lot worse to play against him. Eddie liked to hit guys hard, often with his fists. Still, he did what that Melville coach asked. Winnipeg took advantage and knocked him unconscious. Three times. He lost six teeth and broke both his nose and his jaw. But even then his team won the game, thanks, in part, to Eddie's ferocious discipline.

Eddie had a total belief that he could do anything, and that he was always right. He didn't yell it and scream it; he just insisted and got on with it. So, he thought of himself as a kind of medic, who would massage his hockey battle wounds so that he wouldn't have scars, which he pretty much accomplished. He eventually made it to the NHL with the Boston Bruins. In the 1925–26 season, during a practice, Shore collided so violently with another player that his ear was nearly ripped off. The doctors he saw wanted to amputate it, but he finally found one who agreed to reattach it. He even rejected the anesthetic so that he could watch through a mirror as the doctor sewed his ear back on, Eddie directing the stitching.

He was also at the center of one of the most infamous incidents in the early years of the NHL. In Boston Garden on December 12, 1933, Shore hit Toronto Maple Leafs star Ace Bailey from behind, mistakenly thinking it had been Bailey who'd knocked him to the ice moments earlier. Bailey's head hit the ice so hard he started to convulse, and he nearly died.

Ace Bailey had a fractured skull. After four hours of surgery, it was touch and go whether he would live. But he survived, and a few months later he even shook Shore's hand at the benefit game the NHL held at Maple Leaf Gardens to raise money for Bailey and his family. It would represent the league's first All-Star Game, something that wouldn't be formally introduced for another thirteen years. Ace Bailey never played another game in the NHL.

Eddie Shore certainly did. And he was much more than a rough-and-tumble menace on the ice. He became one of the best defensemen in the game's history, winning the Stanley Cup with the Bruins in 1929 and 1939 and the Hart Memorial Trophy as the NHL's Most Valuable Player four times, in 1933, 1935, 1936, and 1938, which remains a record for a defenseman. He was inducted into the Hockey Hall of Fame in its first year of existence, 1947, and into Canada's Sports Hall of Fame in 1975. In January 2017 Shore was named one of the "100 Greatest NHL Players" in history. So he certainly was a great talent on the ice.

By the time I caught up with him he was the fifty-six-year-old boss of the Springfield Indians. His reputation as a, shall we say, highly unorthodox owner was such that coaches used to threaten to send "problem" players to Eddie Shore to make them learn how to respect authority. Or just to drive them crazy.

Some of the things Shore did were bonkers. He called us all "Mister" and was very polite, but it only made his craziness louder. He'd act as a chiropractor, even though he wasn't, and so would end up injuring the players he treated. He'd make us practice in the dark to save electricity. He'd make his goalies use skates that didn't fit instead of buying them new ones. More than a few goalies lost their toenails as a result.

He insisted that players skate in a kind of "sitting" position, with your knees bent and exactly eleven inches apart. He'd open a training camp by ordering players to tap dance in the hotel lobby or do ballet steps on ice. He'd tape a player's hands to his stick if he thought he was holding it the "wrong" way (i.e., not how Eddie would hold it).

When his players weren't in the lineup he'd make them work the concessions: popping popcorn, blowing up balloons, selling programs. He was so tight with a dollar that guys who had bonus clauses for scoring twenty goals would be benched when they got close. Once he even traded a player for a hockey net, then complained that the net was used.

So that was Eddie Shore. He sure didn't think much of me, either. Not because of race; it was just Eddie.

Before my first game for the Indians, I warmed up, preparing to go in and save the day—and then sat on the bench for the rest of the game. Eddie had handed Punch the head coaching reins but was still calling a lot of the shots. And one of those shots kept me plastered to the bench.

It was the same thing for the next four games.

In the sixth game, at the fourteen-minute mark in the third period, one of our guys got hurt. Shore finally told Imlach to put me on. Not having played for five and two-thirds games, I wasn't exactly in my best game-shape, but I was keen to show Shore what I could do. Plus I was just really annoyed with him.

So with anger fueling my jets I charged out there and sped after the puck—and promptly tripped on a piece of debris, tumbling to the ice. I guess Eddie thought that meant I couldn't skate at all, so he had me pulled from the game. The next morning he told me I was going back to Quebec.

I was very happy to be getting out of Shore's Springfield Lunatic Asylum, but I was also angry. He had insulted my professional pride. "What did you bring me down here for if you were just going to leave me on the bench?" I asked him.

His reply was classic Eddie Shore: "You can't skate right, you can't play with the puck, you can't backcheck right. I thought you were a better hockey player."

I was astonished. He hadn't even seen me play. So I reminded him of that fact and then got on the train, vowing I'd do anything I could to avoid ever playing for Eddie Shore again.

I returned to the Aces with fire inside me, having been embarrassed by my lack of playing time in Springfield. But then a different emergency came up, and things changed very much for the better.

In January 1958 the Quebec Aces got a phone call from the Boston Bruins: one of their forwards had been injured and they needed a player for a back-to-back series against the Montreal Canadiens. And the player they needed was me.

I knew that the injured guy was soon to return and that I wouldn't be needed for long, but that didn't matter at all. I was going to the NHL for the very first time. And I believed that once they saw me play, I'd be back.

I was so excited I could hardly sleep the Friday night before the game, playing it in every possible way in my head. When I took the train the next morning from Quebec City to Montreal, I got a bit of rest on the way. Then I met the Bruins at the Mount Royal Hotel.

My first NHL game would be in the fabled Montreal Forum, which of course I knew well, having played in it for nearly two years with the Quebec Aces. Just the week before, we'd played there against the Montreal Royals. It was a handsome building—state-of-the-art when it went up in 1924—that had seen some of the game's greatest players wearing the home colors, among them Georges Vezina, Howie Morenz, and my hero, Rocket Richard. And the Forum had its own Stanley Cup banners, nine of them hanging from the ceiling, the Canadiens' most recent one from the preceding season when they beat the Bruins in the finals.

In fact, the Bruins hadn't won the Stanley Cup since 1941. They had a talented lineup, but the Original Six NHL was tight, and one position could make or break a team. Even top goalies couldn't always bring it home. For example, back in the 1940s Boston had Frankie Brimsek in goal—known as "Mister Zero" on account of his famous shutout game—and when I made my debut they had Harry Lumley. Now, Lumley had won the Hart Trophy as NHL MVP and the Vezina Trophy as the league's top goalie, and yet the year before it still hadn't been quite enough to get past the Montreal Canadiens for the Cup.

But tonight I was about to play against the Canadiens themselves, so I sure had butterflies in my stomach. The Bruins and I both knew I was just plugging a gap, but they treated me as if I were the team MVP. Don McKenney, a tall, elegant centerman and, as I've mentioned, the nicest guy—in 1960 he'd win the Lady Byng for his gentlemanly play—welcomed me into the dressing room, setting the tone for the rest of the guys. It felt as if I'd always been a Bruin.

And so I was, on January 18, 1958. And the game would be televised on *Hockey Night in Canada*, the broadcast that captured the attention of the entire country every Saturday night, the one I'd grown up listening to on the radio.

Plus, my parents and some of my friends had traveled to Montreal for the game and were as excited as I was. It took us all back to when I'd first played in an organized league as a five-year-old, Harry and Rosebud jumping up and down at rinkside to stay warm. Now they were jumping with joy, as were my pals Junior and Bubsy. I saw how much my achievement meant to them all, and it certainly meant the world to me.

As for the world itself, there was no mention in the news media that I was going to be doing something historic when I stepped out onto the ice of the Montreal Forum. It wasn't the first thing in my mind either, to be honest. I was now an NHL player who happened to be black. History, of course, would make much more of it than we did on that night. All I wanted to do was play my best against the best team in the NHL.

Bruins coach Milt Schmidt told me that, even though I would attract attention, not to worry about it—to focus on playing the game they knew I could play so well, and not on "anything else." I knew he meant fans yelling insults or the opposing players taking shots, but that hadn't worried me in the minors and it wasn't going to worry me now.

The Montreal Canadiens were in the middle of their five consecutive Stanley Cups run, and playing against them would be like playing against the Hockey Hall of Fame. There was Jean Béliveau, the former star of the Quebec Aces. To score a goal I'd have to get the puck past Jacques Plante, one of the greatest goalies of all time. After, of course, getting myself past Doug Harvey on defense, one of the finest d-men ever to play the game. Rocket Richard was out with injuries, so I didn't get to share the ice with him, but I got to be on it with his younger brother Henri, known as the Pocket Rocket.

The Bruins, despite their middle-of-the-pack record, had talent too. Fernie Flaman was a wonderful defenseman—he wasn't big but he had speed and a very good hockey brain, and he was our captain. Fleming Mackell was a fast center. Leo Boivin was a defenseman you could always count on to make the smart play.

It's funny how quickly what once had seemed a faraway dream can become ordinary, and by "ordinary" I mean something you're just supposed to do. So I wasn't sitting in the dressing room all starry-eyed about my teammates. I was sitting in the dressing room as a part of a team. Even so, there were guys sitting next to me whom I'd admired for a while now. I smiled to myself at being in the same room with Johnny Bucyk, Leo Boivin, and Allan Stanley, players who would make it to the Hall of Fame. They all knew me from training camp because I'd played with them in the pre-season. It was Bucyk who said, "We've got your back, and just play your game. You're a Bruin now." I felt very good. These guys were sincere and wanted me to do well.

And near the end of the first period, it was Bucyk—a talented left-winger who'd joined the Bruins the previous year in a trade with Detroit for Terry Sawchuk, one of the greatest goalies of all time—who opened the scoring for us. Then, in the middle of the second, Larry Regan—a magical right-wing puck handler who, at twenty-seven, had joined the team as one of the oldest NHL rookies of 1956—put us up 2–0. Finally Bronco Horvath—in his first season with the Bruins, and a centerman who could find the back of the net in his sleep—got one of the thirty goals he would notch that season when he made it 3–0 for us in the third period.

I nearly got a goal as well in that period when Jerry Toppazzini—a popular, grinding right-winger and one of the best forecheckers I ever saw—put a beautiful pass on my stick as I cruised in on Jacques Plante. However, Montreal defenseman Tom Johnson hooked me and took the edge off my shot. Plante made a stick save and Johnson got a two-minute penalty. We didn't need another goal that night, but it would have been great to stamp a big exclamation mark on my debut with one in the back of the Habs net.

Montreal lost only seventeen games that season and would go on to win the 1958 Stanley Cup, beating Boston again in the final. But they couldn't solve the Bruins on the night I made history—not on the score sheet, yet, but in the story of the game.

A reporter from Montreal's CFCF television station interviewed me. When he asked how it felt to play for the Boston

Bruins, I told him it was the greatest thrill of my life. Neither of us mentioned the history I was making on that night. To be honest, I wasn't even thinking of it. He must have been, as a reporter, but he never brought it up. *Hockey Night in Canada* didn't mention it either, and instead focused on the prime minister of Laos, Prince Souvanna Phouma, who was on a state visit to Canada and was a guest at that game.

Afterward I met up with my parents and Junior and Bubsy. They were even more excited now as we talked about what it had been like to face the mighty Canadiens—it's always better when you win—but we didn't have much time together, since the Bruins had to make the train back to Boston for the Sunday rematch against Montreal. So it was hugs and handshakes and then I was on my way.

Not gone, though: my name had been forever etched in the story of the National Hockey League. Even if they hadn't quite registered it yet.

The New York Times, I found out later, had in fact announced my historic appearance, on page 20, in one short wire-service paragraph headlined "Negro Skater Will Debut as Bruins' Wing":

> *The Boston Bruins today called up a left wing, Billy O'Ree, from Quebec to bolster their sagging team for a week-end home-and-home series with the Montreal Canadiens. O'Ree will be the first Negro to play in a National Hockey League game.*

Wherever I played, I was usually the first black player fans had ever seen, and that usually made things harder—sometimes a little, sometimes a lot. There were times when I considered quitting. But I'll never forget one afternoon in Kingston, Ontario, where I was playing for the Frontenacs. I bought lemonade from a stand set up by a couple of little boys. As I walked away, I heard one say: "That's Willie O'Ree!" Something in his voice told me that while I often stood out from the other players, there was admiration and respect, more often than there were uglier things, and that kept me going.

No one ever made it to the NHL without a strong family making sacrifices and offering support. I was lucky in that regard. At the top, that's my niece and me in a rare moment when I wasn't chasing a ball or puck. In the middle, that's me outside the house I grew up in. And at the bottom, those are my parents Harry and Rosebud in the middle. They were strict but fair, and my friends just adored my mother. That's my sister Margaret and her husband on the left, and my brother Richard and his wife on the right.

I always give my brother Richard special credit for helping me make it to the NHL. We would practice together, and he would play as rough and tough as any brother in the history of hockey. If I ever complained, he'd just say, "They hit harder than that in the NHL!" When I got there, I was ready. That's him in the upper left of the top photo. And that's the two of us sharing a laugh years later. As you can see, he was a pretty big guy.

I got into my fair share of trouble as a kid, but no one can say I wasn't a choirboy. That's me in the school choir in the back row of the top photo—though I also sang at church. And I worked hard at school too. My parents saw to that. The rule: whatever you do, do the best you can.

There's more to life than hockey. Like rugby and baseball, for example. I would play any sport there was to play (with the occasional break to go fishing). I got good enough at baseball to be invited to the Milwaukee Braves training camp in 1956. Camp was in Waycross, Georgia—deep in the Jim Crow South. That trip really opened my eyes to the grim realities of segregation. When I left Georgia I had to sit at the back of the bus. By the time I got home, I was sitting at the front. I decided that day to focus on hockey.

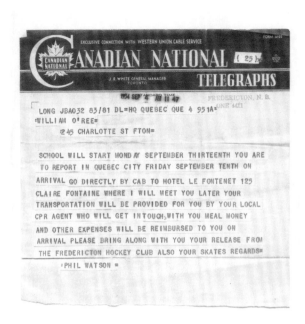

CANADIAN NATIONAL TELEGRAPHS

I still have the telegram that changed my life, and turned me into a professional hockey player. I was thrilled to head to Quebec City to join the Aces. I loved the city, the hockey was fast and tough, and it proved to me that I belonged. The fact that superstars like Jean Béliveau had played there made the move that much more exciting, as did the fact that black superstar Herb Carnegie had played there with him. Béliveau said that Carnegie was one of the best he had ever played with, but Carnegie never made it to the NHL.

© Macdonald Stewart/Hockey Hall of Fame

My time in Quebec changed not only my life, but also my family's. I was putting up the kind of numbers that showed NHL decision-makers that I had what it took to play in the world's best league. And I was making enough money to send a little home to my parents, who were able to buy their first house.

On January 18, 1958, my dream came true. I was called up from the Aces to play against the Canadiens at the Forum in Montreal. There could hardly be a better stage for the most exciting moment of a young man's life. I found out only later that *The New York Times* had been watching the Bruins' moves, and had announced my first game before it even happened: "O'Ree will be the first Negro to play in a National Hockey League game."

Hockey is a team sport, and whether you win or lose depends a lot on how well you play together. Good teams stick up for each other, too. Hockey can be rough, but it can also bring the best out in people. It meant a lot to me to be part of that Bruins team. In the photo below, that's me with my line-mates, Tom McCarthy and Charlie Burns.

To Willie
The Greatest
Best Wishes Always
Milt Schmidt
10-26-07

A lot of guys' careers were shaped by Milt Schmidt, who was a legend in his own right. He was an NHL All-Star, a bona fide war hero, a coach, and later a Stanley Cup-winning general manager. He was also a consummate gentleman. When he was asked about dressing the first black player in NHL history, he would say "He's not black. He's a Bruin." Though we might not phrase things the same way today, I knew what he meant—that the colour of my skin didn't matter. All that mattered was my role on the team. That was all I asked for, and I appreciated it. I did face some ugly racism while I was wearing a Bruins sweater, and Schmidt always had my back.

I don't think any hockey player's wife would say the constant travel is the best way to keep a relationship strong and stable. But I met Deljeet while I was playing on the west coast, and we've been together ever since. She's had my back just as bravely as any linemate.

WILLIE O'REE

LOS ANGELES
BLADES

My time in the NHL was shorter than I'd hoped— likely because of an injury to my eye. But I had a lot of hockey left in me, and a lot of goals. I was traded to the Los Angeles Blades, and later went to the San Diego Gulls. Life in California was so good that I've never really left.

One of the reasons I think it is so important for kids to have the opportunity to play hockey is that sport is the beginning of so many friendships (whether you're wearing the same sweater or not!). Friendship is not just sharing a laugh, it's also going the extra mile for each other. One guy who was both a teammate and a friend was Bruins great Johnny Bucyk, who was always a leader, and always made me feel welcome. In the middle photo, that's Neil Henderson with Lou Vairo, Sam Greenblatt, and me. And in the bottom photo that's me with old Fredericton pals Johnny and Gus Mazzuca—that's my nephew Stephen O'Ree between them. After all these years, they're still not Bruins fans.

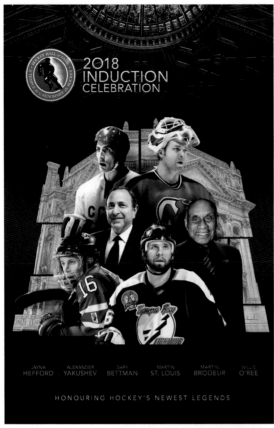

JAYNA HEFFORD | ALEXANDER YAKUSHEV | GARY BETTMAN | MARTIN ST. LOUIS | MARTIN BRODEUR | WILLIE O'REE

© Hockey Hall of Fame

It was a long time ago that I listened to "Hockey Night in Canada" on the radio with my family. I dreamt of being out there on the ice with my heroes, but I don't think I ever imagined being in the Hockey Hall of Fame. Some of those heroes, like Maurice Richard and Jean Beliveau, are there now. And as of November 2018, I am too, along with incredible players like Martin St. Louis, Martin Brodeur, Russian legend Alexander Yakushev, and Jenna Hefford, and a man who made a big difference in my life, Gary Bettman. Here we all are at the induction ceremony.

© THE CANADIAN PRESS/Nathan Denette

© THE CANADIAN PRESS/Justin Tang

Hockey has given me a lot in life, and many, many people have helped me along the way. I believe that if you've been lucky enough to have people give you a hand, you need to extend that hand to others. That's what I have tried to do over the years. Here I am with some young high school students as part of Black History Month. And in the photo below, that's me in front of the sports complex named after me in my home-town. It is an incredible feeling to know that my name, and the name of my ancestors, will be part of young athletes' lives for many years to come.

After my playing career was over, I always wanted to find a way to get back into the game. When Bryant McBride was putting together an NHL program to make hockey more inclusive, my name came up, and we've been working together ever since. This is a program from a weekend we put together to give kids who might not otherwise be encouraged to play a chance to try it out. We really enjoyed the weekend, but there was a cloud hanging over it, because the KKK threatened to bomb it.

When I was a kid, I dreamt of making it to the NHL. Now I feel as though I made it to the NHL twice—I made it once as a player, and I made it back as an executive. I am incredibly proud of both accomplishments, and I am particularly happy that I have tried to make a difference in young people's lives. As I've said, no one makes it without a helping hand, and I would be thrilled if I helped a young person or two along their paths in life. Here I am with a couple of pretty good hockey players—Anson Carter and Ray Bourque, who are presenting me with my old Number 22 Bruins sweater. It was a long and fantastic road back.

A couple of days later I read about it in *The Globe and Mail*, Canada's biggest newspaper, whose headline read "First Negro to Perform in the NHL, Willie O'Ree Thrilled, Nervous."

Yes, I was thrilled to be playing in the NHL, and I'd certainly been nervous, especially in the first period when my adrenaline was pumping faster than ever, just as the game was faster than I'd ever played it. But my speed was as good as—if not better than—any skater on the ice, and I'd gotten used to playing left wing with a blind right eye. So I'd just gone out and played as I usually played: hard.

It was the last paragraph of that *Globe and Mail* piece, though, that gave me pause. It reads:

> *O'Ree is one of several Negroes to perform in minor league hockey, but his debut in the NHL marks the lowering of the last color line among major sports in North America. However, most hockey observers point out that the only reason a "color line" existed was the fact that there hasn't been a Negro player qualified to make the National Hockey League. Several Negro hockey players have played in the minors, in fact. O'Ree has been a linemate of one—Stan Maxwell.*

A little over two weeks later, Len Bramson wrote in *The Hockey News* that "the fact that there has never been a Negro player in the NHL before O'Ree must be blamed on the Negro race itself."

Of course, there I would strongly beg to differ. As I said earlier in my story, Herb Carnegie could have broken through the so-called "color line" back in 1948, but the New York Rangers' offer wasn't better than the money he was making in the minors, nor did they assure him of a spot. And his brother Ossie and linemate Manny McIntyre were also good enough to crack the NHL. Stan Maxwell could have easily played in the league, too, but he was never offered a contract. It was one of the realities of the Original Six, where there were just so many good players who never got their shot.

There were also Art Dorrington and John Utendale, black players who'd both caught the NHL's attention. Dorrington came from Truro, Nova Scotia, like Stan Maxwell. He played center in what was then the Eastern Amateur Hockey League and in the International Hockey League, suiting up for the Atlantic City Sea Gulls, Johnstown Jets, Washington Lions, and Philadelphia Ramblers. Dorrington notched 163 goals and 157 assists in 345 minor pro games, and he was so good that in 1950 the New York Rangers signed him to a professional contract. But like so many other talented players, he toiled in the minors until he was drafted into the army in 1956. He spent nearly two years in uniform before playing a few games for the Philadelphia Ramblers of the Eastern Hockey League. Then he broke his leg, which ended his career. He never did get called up to the Rangers.

John Utendale, a right-winger from Edmonton, began playing for the Edmonton Oil Kings during high school and then for another two years before signing a contract with the Detroit Red Wings. (I played with him on the Quebec Aces for five games in 1958–59.) Like Dorrington and Maxwell, John never got the call to actually play an NHL game.

So, within my lifetime, there had been at least seven black players good enough to get signed by NHL teams, and yet only one of us had made it to the Big Time. In 1950, *Ebony* magazine, which began life in 1945 for the African American market, ran a piece called "Can Negroes Crack Big League Hockey?" Clarence Campbell, the NHL's president, responded that "the National Hockey League only has one policy: to get the best hockey players. There is no [policy], tacit or otherwise, which would restrict anyone because of color or race."

Today that strikes me as, at best, corporate spin. Of course there were black players good enough to make the NHL at the time—they'd even been offered NHL contracts. And it took eight years from that misleading pronouncement for me to play two games with the Boston Bruins.

The second game, back in Boston, felt much different to me. I mean, it was the NHL, but I wasn't as nervous this time. Now I was Willie O'Ree, NHL veteran. The fans were great, cheering us on just as Boston fans do, no matter what. No jeers were sent my way that night, or on any other night that I played in Boston.

We went into the third period tied at 1, but the Canadiens scored five on us and we lost 6–2. Béliveau got a couple and so did Bernie "Boom Boom" Geoffrion, who was one of the first players to turn the slapshot into a weapon. Montreal just outclassed us. But I didn't feel as if all of a sudden I was in over my head. I played hard, did what I was supposed to do, and didn't lose the game for the Bruins. The Canadiens beat us. That's the nature of sports at any level, and in the six-team NHL, every loss was magnified. And now that I'd been given my shot with the NHL, this one-eyed left-winger knew he could belong there.

I returned to the minors after that night. The Aces ended up finishing in second-last place, with sixty-two points. But that didn't mean we'd had a bad season—the second-place team, Shawinigan, had sixty-seven points. It was a tight league. Still, I'd gotten a taste of the best hockey league in the world, and that's what I was thinking about as the season ended. I wanted to rejoin the Bruins. And deep inside my twenty-two-year-old-heart, I knew I'd be back.

10.

BECOMING A BRUIN

That summer I was home again in Fredericton when Junior and Bubsy and I got involved in what ended up to be a pretty funny incident. It started while we were on our way to my brother's place to play some cards, each of us driving separately. Just as we were all going over the old Carleton Street Bridge, the car in front of Bubsy's veered and sideswiped an oncoming car. Then it just kept on going.

So, while Bubsy went to find the police, Junior and I followed the guy. Not long after Bubsy was able to join us again, Junior finally managed to cut the guy off. Then, when the police arrived, the hit-and-run driver got out of his car and practically slid down the side of it. He was drunk.

We all had to go to court to testify. The guy had hired a pretty slick lawyer, who claimed that the police had smelled alcohol on his client only because he'd drunk "one beer" at the Air Force Club. (Which would have been a record for restraint at that club, known for its conviviality.) The lawyer also criticized the police for putting the guy in a jail cell instead of taking him to the hospital—a pretty impressive bit of fact fiddling, given that the guy hadn't been injured.

When I was called to testify, I told the court that I'd followed the accused after he hit the other car, and that Junior had done the same. It was when they put Bubsy on the stand that things got interesting.

When the prosecutor asked him what he'd seen, Bubsy replied that the hit-and-run driver was clearly drunk. The defense lawyer objected—Bubsy couldn't say that because he didn't know it—and the judge agreed, telling Bubsy that since he wasn't an expert he had to limit his testimony to what he'd seen. To which Bubsy replied, "Well, if he wasn't drunk then he had an epileptic fit."

The courtroom busted up laughing. The judge quieted everyone and the questions continued. Finally, the prosecutor asked Bubsy to show the court exactly what he'd seen when the hit-and-run driver got out of his car. So Bubsy opened the witness stand's gate, took a step forward and fell on the floor, tried to pull himself up onto the stand, then finally slid back down. By this time the courtroom was howling.

The hit-and-run driver was convicted. It turned out that he was a big player in provincial politics: head of Fish and Game for the New Brunswick government. He lost his license for six months.

As we were leaving the courtroom, the policeman who'd arrested the driver told Bubsy that they could never have won the case without him. Then, when the court clerk gave us fifteen dollars each for our time, Bubsy exclaimed that this was as much as he made in a week—and that, if they could swing it, he'd come in every single day to testify on anything else they might want him to testify on.

We all had a great laugh over that. Junior and I still do. Bubsy, such a great friend and athlete but also a heavy smoker, died of lung cancer a few years ago. I can hear his laugh still.

In the middle of that summer of 1958 I got another letter from the Bruins, inviting me back to training camp. Stan Maxwell got a letter too—so again we dared to dream: maybe this time, once the 1958–59 hockey season had begun, we'd both catch on with the team. And I'd be coming in as a guy who'd managed to play in the NHL, not some wet-behind-the-ears rookie out of Quebec. I wasn't quite a grizzled veteran, but I felt like a player who the team knew, someone they'd wanted back. And I understood what it took.

It was great to see Johnny Bucyk and Vic Stasiuk and Bronco Horvath and of course the always welcoming Don McKenney—guys I'd played with on the ice of the Boston Garden and the Montreal Forum. And it was great to be back there with my good friend Stan, who always had my back, just as I had his. It wasn't because we were both black, either; it was more that we'd both come from large Maritime families and knew how lucky we were to be here. When I went to

Boston for training camp in September 1958, I felt confident about making the team because the Bruins knew what I could do. Boston had lost four games to two against the Montreal Canadiens in that year's finals, and I figured I could be the missing piece who'd get them next year's Stanley Cup win.

But general manager Lynn Patrick felt differently: when camp was over, Stan and I once again got sent back to Quebec for more "seasoning." I was really disappointed by this, especially since the guys on the team had made it seem as if I were there to stay. No one said that to me directly, but I just had a great feeling that I was one of them. Johnny and Don would always invite me to join them for a bite to eat and a beer or two, and I'd already imagined doing that as we made our way through the 1958–59 NHL season. Instead I was going back to Quebec.

That 1958–59 season with the Aces I got seasoned pretty good, scoring nine goals and adding twenty-one assists—all while racking up seventy-four minutes in penalties, what with everyone wanting to prove themselves against the guy who'd played in the NHL. Hockey players know who's on the ice at all times. They know your résumé. They know your reputation. And the better your reputation, the harder they come after you. That goes for tough guys and skill guys and everyone in between. They don't leave you alone until you're a legend, and I was far from being a legend. But I was worth coming after, since anyone who could get the better of me could say he'd gotten the better of an NHLer. So I had to be ready. But that was fine by me. I was ready.

———

Then, in July 1959, the Quebec Hockey League announced it would fold. The Quebec Aces and the Chicoutimi Saguenéens both said they would "suspend" operations, which meant they'd shut down, perhaps for good.

But the remaining two teams, the Montreal Royals and the Trois-Rivières Lions, joined up with two teams from the Ontario Hockey Association's Senior Eastern division (the Hull-Ottawa Canadians and the Kingston Merchants, later renamed Frontenacs) and two teams from the OHA's Senior Northern division (the Sudbury Wolves and the Sault Ste. Marie Greyhounds, later renamed Thunderbirds) to form the Eastern Professional Hockey League. In fact, the EPHL was created as the first farm league fully run and controlled by the NHL—and meant to be its primary development league. However, the Detroit Red Wings didn't participate until 1963, which would be the EPHL's final season, and the Toronto Maple Leafs never joined at all.

I wound up playing for the Frontenacs in Kingston, a pretty city on Lake Ontario, about halfway between Toronto and Montreal. At the time, the population was a little more than 400,000, most of them hockey fans. Kingston was, and remains, a first-class hockey town.

I had a great season there playing with Cal Gardner, who was also the coach and whom I'd met briefly in Springfield when he assisted Punch Imlach (and when he played for the team there as well, while keeping out of Eddie Shore's way). Cal had also played for New York, Toronto, Chicago, and Boston. The fact that he'd had so much NHL experience made me think the EPHL really would be my launch pad to a permanent place in the NHL. And although the team finished in last place that 1959–60 season, with twenty-eight wins, thirty-nine losses, and three ties, I had my best year as a pro so far, scoring twenty-one goals and adding twenty-five assists for a total of forty-six points.

Off the ice, my life took a turn I had not expected, but certainly welcomed. During that season, I roomed with the McDonald family. A frequent guest at their house was a pretty young woman named Lynn Campbell, who worked in the business office at Queen's University. She lived about three blocks away and was friends with the McDonalds' daughter. And then she was friends with me. Lynn, a dynamic brunette, was not only very attractive but also a great hockey fan. Before too long, we were dating. She was my first serious girlfriend. She was also white.

Now, my parents were of the old school, believing that you had to marry within your race, especially if you were black. "What would people say if they saw you with a white girl?" was how they viewed it, meaning I'd be letting myself in for abuse from racists. And while I told my parents a lot about my life (except for my blind eye, which they went to their graves none the wiser about), Lynn didn't even mention me to her own, feeling that our relationship wasn't their business anyway. I agreed. We weren't living in the Deep South. Race relations weren't perfect in Canada, but they certainly weren't as terrible as they were in the USA. We were also adults and did not need permission to live or love from anyone.

At one point, when I was back home in Fredericton after my first season, I asked my mother if she'd like to come with me on my visit to Kingston to see Lynn. She agreed, and the three of us had a very pleasant time. But I could see that my mother was unhappy. It's not what eventually ended my relationship with Lynn—that would be the fact that I left Kingston—but it certainly sat uneasily with me. I respected my parents, and although they'd raised me to live my own life, I knew that the bigotry they had experienced growing up was still with us. If Lynn and I were to get married and start a family, did I want to put our children into what I might have seen at the time as a disadvantage? Or worse, something that would cause them pain?

Lynn and I later broke up for a variety of reasons. We did meet again about forty years later, when she attended the screening of a film about my life and came to the party afterward. It was nice to see her. But I live my life going forward, and I had no regrets.

During that summer of 1960 in Fredericton, I often wondered if I'd regret not getting the chance to play in the NHL again before I got too old. I was twenty-four, and it was getting to be now-or-never time.

I was out walking one day, thinking about my future, when I turned down George Street and saw that two boys, who looked to be around eight, had opened a lemonade stand. The street was so empty you could have fired a cannon down its length and maybe grazed a squirrel, but these boys had still gone to all this trouble to set up their stand. So I stopped and bought a glass, wanting to make them feel their work had been worth it. Also, I was thirsty.

Afterward, when I was walking away, I heard one boy say to the other, "Do you know who that was? That was Willie O'Ree. He plays for the Boston Bruins!"

Hearing the wonder in that boy's voice, and his belief that I was still a Bruin, resonated with me more than any coach's pep talk ever could. I felt it was a kind of omen, and that I would indeed be a Boston Bruin again soon.

The second call from Boston came in December. "Just bring your skates," the Bruins told me. It meant they were going to provide me with equipment and sticks. It meant I'd be staying in Boston for a while.

It meant I was on the team.

So I took the train down to Boston. This time I'd be living with my mother's cousin Edith out in the suburb of Roxbury, home at the time mainly to black people. I'd commute into the city on a train about three-quarters full of black people, practice with the team or play games, and then return to Roxbury. It was just how life was in Boston. And it seemed normal, since I was living with family. Roxbury's large West Indian and Caribbean population meant that the local food was very much of the islands, as were the sports—they were mad about cricket and puzzled about hockey.

But I was about to get the chance to educate them. That's because, one week before Christmas 1960, I got the best Christmas present ever: I was now back in the Bruins' black and gold, and looked to be staying for good.

—

I was now, officially, the first black player in the NHL—although, once again, the white media didn't make a big deal of that fact. The black media, however, took notice. I hoped that if you were a black kid playing hockey, hearing about me would make you play harder so that you too could one day join the NHL. But again, I was a hockey player who happened to be black, and not, in my mind, a black hockey player.

My coach, Milt Schmidt, used to have a standard line when speaking to the media about my being a different shade of human from the other guys on the team. "He isn't black," Schmidt would say, "he's a Bruin."

Nice to hear, but I was still one of the few black people at Boston Garden—and I was playing! Not many black people went to games in those days. The Bruins were great about getting players tickets when we needed them, though, so I was able to increase the Garden's black attendance by giving tickets to my cousin and her friends, along with people in Roxbury generally. Now all those cricket-mad West Indians could see what the blue line was, how you couldn't cross it ahead of the puck, and so on. To me, hockey is far easier to grasp than cricket, and the good people of Roxbury soon caught on.

My parents came to see me play, and so did my brother Richard. I was so proud when the guy who'd given me such rough-and-tumble hockey tutorials saw me wearing the black and gold, my number 22 on the back. All those dreams I'd told Richard about on Island Lake and on the ice rinks of Fredericton had come true.

I loved life in the NHL, pro hockey's greatest realm, because I'd made my dream come true. They could have made us *walk* to away games and I'd still have been over the moon.

On the road I roomed with centerman Charlie Burns, easily the most popular player with the home crowd. In those days he was unique in being the NHL's only American-born player (later, as a child, his family had moved to Toronto and he became a Canadian). Not only was he a great skater and playmaker, he could play a defensive as well as an offensive game. Charlie also had a great sense of humor and a fine mind for strategy. He could "see the ice," as they say, and talk about how to get around opponents' defenses in a way that made him sound like a coach—which is what he eventually became. In fact, with the Minnesota North Stars, he was the last to hold a dual player-coach role in the NHL.

He also wore a thickly padded helmet at a time when no one wore helmets at all. In junior hockey he'd suffered a head injury that nearly ended his career, but the doctors put a metal plate in his head and Charlie returned to the game. We were a pair: him with a plate in his head and me with one eye. Of course, no one on the Bruins knew about my blind eye. At least not yet.

We formed a line, with Charlie as centerman and Jerry Toppazzini on right wing, and we were friends off the ice as well. Topper, who came from Sudbury, had a nose for where to find good Italian food in all our away cities—and in his retirement he would start a Bruins-themed restaurant.

I loved traveling on the rails to New York and Chicago and Detroit and Toronto and Montreal. In those days teams would play back-to-back games in each other's rinks, so we'd go back and forth on the train together. And since there were only six teams, rivalries were intense. I mean, imagine being on the same train with a guy you'd dropped the gloves with just a couple of hours earlier. We kept to our separate railcars, but you could bump into the other teams on the way to the dining car. It could get testy. Mostly, though, we had fun with the guys on our own team. We'd play cards—hearts, say, or rummy; we'd tell stories, many of them true; and we'd kid around with each other about shots we'd missed, as hockey players do.

The thing I loved most about being an NHLer was getting to play against some of the best guys in hockey. I remember being on the ice against Gordie Howe in Detroit. He was six one and just over two hundred pounds and he was a beast. Built like a heavyweight champion, he could fight like one, too. And on January 16, 1960, the guy you saw on the ice making plays happen out of nothing became the NHL's career-scoring leader when he passed my hero Rocket Richard's 946 points.

But Howe also had windshield-wiper elbows that he used like an artist—you didn't want to get into corners with him, or get too close period, or those elbows would be right in your face, giving it a wash. He may have been nicknamed Mr. Hockey, but he was also called Mr. Elbows. (A "Gordie Howe hat trick" is a goal, an assist, and a fight all in the same game, which should give you a sense of the kind of mixture of skill and toughness he brought.)

I was on the third line and Gordie was on a line all his own, so we never really saw ice time against each other. I'd watch him from the bench, though, and marvel at what a complete hockey player he was—one who could skate and shoot and hit and dangle the puck as if it were on a string, and then put it in the net whenever he wanted to, so it seemed, without ever seeming to break a sweat. Some guys are always churning—you can *see* how hard they're working. But Gordie just seemed to glide. Even when teams tried (unwisely) to play physically with Mr. Hockey, he'd just calmly shrug them off. He seemed unhurried and graceful, as though he were playing a slightly different game from the rest of us. When the Rocket retired, he said Gordie was better than he was. "He can do everything." And that was saying something.

I also liked Terry Sawchuk, who played goal for the Red Wings. Most nights the puck looked like a beach ball to Sawchuk. He could stop everything. He was fearless. And he didn't wear a mask, either.

It's shocking to think how unprotected we were back then, with no helmets or visors, but goalies were even less protected. If you compare a photo of Terry Sawchuk in 1960 with any goalie today, the modern players look as though they've been pumped up with air like a balloon, they're so padded and protected. And rightly so. The frozen piece of rubber that is a hockey puck, speeding toward your face at a hundred miles an hour, is a dangerous thing. Believe me, I know.

Sawchuk took a lot of pucks to the face, but he was a tough guy. And we had something in common. When he was eighteen a stick caught him in his right eye during a game. The doctor wanted to cut it out but then changed his mind, and a good thing, too; Terry later regained his sight. He went on to win four Vezina Trophies as the NHL's best goalie. He also won four Stanley Cups and posted 103 shutouts in 971 regular-season games. The only goalie who's posted more is Martin Brodeur, and he got his 125 shutouts over 1,266 games.

The Bruins were paying me $9,000 for the season, more than twice what I'd been making in the minor pro leagues. And even though I knew Boston wanted to keep me, I played every game as if it were my last. But I still hadn't put a puck past an NHL goalie.

On New Year's Day, 1961, we were playing at home against Montreal. The Canadiens had won the Stanley Cup the year before (their fifth in a row), and some of the best players to ever play the game remained in their lineup. Boom Boom Geoffrion was smashing pucks into the net that left no doubt about his nickname; close behind him was Jean Béliveau. Rocket Richard had retired, but the Canadiens had a deep bench. They'd also developed a strong farm-team system. It looked as if they'd be unbeatable again that season.

Before that game against the Canadiens, my teammate Bronco Horvath saw me shooting on our goalie, Bruce Gamble, in the pre-game practice. Bronco played center, and the year before he'd come second in the scoring race with thirty-nine goals and forty-one assists in a seventy-game season. So he knew how to put the puck in the net.

"O'Ree," he said, "you're shooting too high. You have to keep your shots low to be effective."

I knew this, but I'd been up against Canadiens netminder Charlie Hodge before, when he'd been the goalie for the Montreal Royals and I played for the Quebec Aces. Charlie was a little guy, maybe five six and 150 pounds, so I'd always shoot high on him. I'd scored in Quebec by going upstairs on Charlie Hodge. I figured I'd do the same that night.

It was a tough game, with both sides fighting hard to kick off the new year and make a statement. Halfway through the third period we had a 2–1 lead. Both teams had a man in the penalty box, so there was quite a bit more space on the ice. I took a pass from Leo Boivin and turned on the speed. I've always been blessed with quick acceleration—a couple of steps and I'd be gone. Milt Schmidt, my coach, thought I was the fastest skater in the league. With open ice I had a lot of room to do my thing, though sometimes I went so fast that with my blind eye I left the puck behind.

But not on this night. I sped by Montreal defenseman Jean-Guy Talbot just inside the Canadiens' blue line. Then Tom Johnson came after me, but he broke his stick trying to stop me. Suddenly I was all alone in front of Charlie Hodge.

I was about to shoot high out of habit when I heard Bronco Horvath's words in my head. So instead I let the puck rip along the ice. It beat Hodge. That sweet red light that signals a goal flashed and nearly fourteen thousand people in Boston Garden were standing and cheering for me. I had finally scored my first NHL goal on the very first day of a new year. That couldn't be anything but a good sign of things to come.

I dove into the net and grabbed the puck, then skated it over to the bench and gave it to Milt Schmidt, asking him to look after it for me. He smiled and promised that he would. I still have that puck at home.

For two minutes afterward, those fourteen thousand people in Boston Garden kept standing and cheering for me. After a while I didn't know where to look. I'd known that the fans in Boston were on my side, but I hadn't realized how much. Milt Schmidt later said that it was the longest ovation he'd ever heard in his twenty-five years being around the Bruins. And he'd been in the Garden on some pretty big nights. They were cheering because I'd scored my first NHL goal, but they were also cheering for history.

And not only was it my first goal, it also turned out to be the game winner. Henri Richard later scored for Montreal to make it 3–2 and a nail-biting finale. But my goal stood.

Back home in Fredericton, my parents heard the news of my goal and of Boston's response. It looked as if their fear of my rejection by the white world of big-league pro hockey had been disproven. I'd been welcomed into the NHL. And I was going to stay welcome for a long time.

In 1961 the civil rights movement was just getting going. The United States had begun to grapple with its original sin of slavery and its subsequent discrimination against black people and people of color generally. I'm sorry to say that the movement hadn't yet reached the pro hockey world. I did get asked about it, though, when I finally made it on to *Hockey Night in Canada* and was interviewed by Ward Cornell.

And midway through that almost five-minute interview, it was I who brought up the elephant in the studio. In recounting my arrival in the NHL I mentioned that my old coach Phil Watson had told me I could be "the Jackie Robinson of hockey."

Ward Cornell was not a flashy interviewer, but he was sharp.

"In terms of this business of being the Jackie Robinson of hockey," he said, his head down, his arms folded across his beefy chest, "have you had any troubles?" We both knew the kind of troubles Robinson had experienced over his entire major league career.

I realized that I could go two ways here. I could tell Ward Cornell about the *"maudit negre"* chants in Quebec, the "Colored Only" Jim Crow restrictions in Georgia, the fact that "troubles" was too mild a word for it. Or I could give him the hockey answer.

You probably know what I mean by "hockey answer." If you're looking for insight into deep questions, don't ask a hockey player with a mic in your hand and the camera rolling. Hockey players tend to say as little as possible, because the less you say, the less you can say wrong. Players worry about saying something the coach won't like. Or even worse, something their opponents *will* like. Remember, hockey players love to get under each other's skin. If I tell the whole league on national television that racial barbs really bother me, I can pretty much guarantee that I'll hear more of them.

After all, if I tell them I've got a sore rib, they're going to hit me every chance they get.

Above all, you want to be team-first. That's just hockey culture. Talking about your own unique challenges is about as far from team-first as you can get. So I gave the hockey answer, and let viewers figure it out for themselves.

"No, none that you could say were troubles," I told him. "I've heard a few jeers, but I guess all hockey players get that."

Which is true, but they didn't get the type of jeers I was getting in some arenas.

And then, ever so casually, Cornell asked me, "When you're on the road, whom do you room with?"

I told him that on the road I roomed with Charlie Burns.

"Good," said Cornell. After that he moved on to the fate of the Bruins: we were sitting in the basement at that point in the season, and it's where we would finish. But this seemingly offhand question about my roommate would have revealed much to an audience at the time, who were well aware of the discrimination many U.S. hotels showed to black people by turning us away at the door. And my answer told everyone that it wasn't a problem for the Bruins, or for me, and shouldn't be one at all.

Indeed, I've never had a problem with any of my teammates on the eleven pro teams I've played for. The guys wearing the same jersey as I wore have been supportive, and considerate, and rooting for me on every single team, no exceptions. The problem was with the players on the other teams.

Now, that doesn't include the Montreal Canadiens or the Toronto Maple Leafs. Canada likes to think of itself as a more tolerant society than the United States, and maybe it is, although, as I've said, I've had my problems at home. I think the real reason I was left alone when Boston played in Canada was that players and fans knew me from my junior and minor pro days. I was a familiar face.

But in the United States, even though all the players were Canadian, I was a black face in a very white game with a very white fan base. I used to hear ugly name-calling in New York, Detroit, and Chicago, from the fans, mainly, but sometimes from the players. Just as Coot had predicted—and prepared me for—players would cross-check me. They'd take runs at me to knock me into the boards. They wanted to see what the black guy would do. And there wasn't a game in my first NHL season when an ugly racial remark wasn't directed at me.

I've said that I let racism go in one ear and out the other, but I heard it all right. And one night, after an opposing player had called me the N-word, I decided to do something about it. I skated up to the referee and told him, "This guy just called me a nasty name." The referee said, "What do you want me to do about it?" and then skated away. I got the message. I'd have to deal with it myself. And so, yes, I had my fair share of fights—never because I wanted to fight but because I had to. Even so, in my 1961 NHL season I racked up only twenty-six minutes of penalties, which was pretty low compared to some of my penalty totals in other leagues I played in. I did have to fight more in the western league, where I played for fourteen years. Guys came after me. But I was also an aggressive player, and that had something to do with it as well.

Today the NHL takes racial incidents very seriously. It's sad to see that racist words and actions still happen, but very good to see how the league responds. Players who insult another player because of his race are punished with heavy fines and are embarrassed in the media. A couple of years ago all five major league teams in Boston joined up to combat racism among fans, so it's still very much with us. Back then, though, I didn't have any official help. I knew I'd have to look after myself.

It was on the ice in Chicago that I had my worst experience with another player. I was excited about playing Chicago Stadium, a large, gorgeous arena, the biggest in the United States when it opened in 1929. And I was excited about playing against the Black Hawks and learning some tricks from their big star, Bobby Hull, a.k.a. the Golden Jet. He was fast, but was he faster than me? I was hoping to find out.

Bobby Hull could certainly shoot the puck harder than I could. His shot was so hard that it scared goalies. Bobby, a left-winger like me, loved to shoot from the slot. He'd won the Art Ross Trophy as the NHL's scoring champion the previous season by firing his cannon from there, and he'd win it twice more before he was finished. In fact, four of the first six fifty-goal seasons in the NHL belong to Bobby Hull. With his blond hair flowing as he made a thrilling end-to-end rush, he was yet another reason why people loved the energy and speed of hockey.

Chicago also had future Hall-of-Famers Glenn Hall in goal and Stan Mikita at center. Hall had reflexes so fast that just when shooters would figure they had him beat, his glove hand would whip out and he'd snatch the puck in midair. He was so nervous before games that he used to throw up, but once he was on the ice he had nerves of steel and that glove hand to match.

Stan Mikita was blessed with many talents on the ice. He won the NHL scoring title four times in five years and the Hart Trophy as the NHL's Most Valuable Player twice. He was also tough, but that's because of his tough childhood. In 1948, when Stan was just eight years old, his parents shipped him out of his native Czechoslovakia, not wanting him to grow up under the communist dictatorship. So Stan came to live with his aunt and uncle in Canada. It was hard enough for me to leave home when I was nineteen to go to another province, so I can't imagine how scared this little kid felt being sent across the world to live with strangers. He didn't speak English and looked like he came from a poor Eastern European country, so the other kids picked on him. Stan fought back, and kept on fighting back, right into the NHL. I knew how he felt. In 1966, his six-year-old daughter, Meg, asked him about his frequent trips to the penalty box. "Daddy, when that guy in the stripes blew the whistle, why did Uncle Bobby [Hull] go sit with his friends and you went all the way across the ice and sat by yourself?" Mikita was so moved by his child's question that he changed his belligerent style and decided to just play hockey. As a result, he won the Lady Byng Trophy the following two seasons for gentlemanly play.

So there I was, in the old Chicago Stadium with all these stars, looking forward to a great game. They played the national anthem on that big Wurlitzer organ, and the fans roared to shake the rafters. That old organ did make the hairs stand up on your neck. It was exhilarating to be there.

But I didn't get to see how I stacked up against Hull. The game was less than two minutes old when trouble hit. It was just the second shift of the first period when Chicago right-winger Eric Nesterenko skated up to me and called me the N-word. Nesterenko was big: six two or three and about two hundred pounds. He was rough, too. His nickname was "Elbows" because he liked to pop guys in the face with them.

So he called me that nasty name, and before I had time to respond, he took his stick and butt-ended me in the mouth. Butt-ending is one of the dirtiest things you can do in hockey. A guy will slide his top hand down, exposing the end of his stick. Then he'll jam that knob into another guy's ribs or, as in my case, his face. Along with slew-footing, the butt-end is about as dirty as hockey gets. The butt-end is nothing more than an attempt to injure another player, and that's what Eric Nesterenko was trying to do to me.

It worked. His butt-end knocked out my two front teeth, split my lip, and broke my nose. Then Nesterenko stood there, smiling, and said the N-word again. I stayed on my feet, though, and stared him down. So he tried to high-stick me. But by that point I'd had enough. I ducked under it and smacked him over the head with my stick. I cut him pretty good—it took fourteen or fifteen stitches to close him up.

Blood was now flowing from my mouth and from his head, but he wasn't ready to quit. He'd thought I would back off, and now he was mad that the black man had fought back, so he went after me. He grabbed me; we went up against the glass. He was bigger than I was, so he had a longer arm reach. I knew I couldn't beat him in a fight because of his size, so I pulled him in close to make sure he couldn't punch me. The safest place in a hockey fight is as close as you can get to the guy who's trying to punch you.

Meanwhile, both benches had cleared and everyone was fighting. The fans were hollering at me because that's what fans do at opposing players. Or maybe a few were hollering at me for daring to play hockey while black.

Finally, the linesmen broke up the brawl. Nesterenko and I each got five-minute penalties for drawing blood and ten-minute misconducts.

They took me to the Boston dressing room to fix me up. They plugged up my broken nose and washed off the blood. I wanted to go back out and play, but the trainer said it was too dangerous. The Chicago officials had said there'd be "injuries" if I went back in, which meant someone might try to kill me. Which is pretty much what I felt Eric Nesterenko had tried to do already.

Chicago believed that they couldn't control their own fans or players, so they locked me in the Boston dressing room for the rest of the game—for my own protection. The room didn't have a TV as they do today, so for nearly the whole game I sat there alone, wondering what was happening out on the ice. So much for seeing Bobby Hull and Stan Mikita and Glenn Hall. I was a prisoner in Chicago Stadium.

After the game, things were still tense. The Chicago officials told us we'd need a police escort to get out of the rink safely. The police marched us to our team bus, but there wasn't any trouble. Eric Nesterenko wasn't out there waiting for me. There was no mob. We got on the bus and safely out of Chicago.

When I spoke to my parents, they told me they'd read all about my fight. But the newspapers didn't tell the whole story. The gist of it was that "Willie O'Ree and Eric Nesterenko had a bloody stick-duel in Chicago." I didn't tell my parents what really happened. And I never did. For the rest of their lives, they never knew the truth. It would have hurt them too much.

I had to go back to Chicago again later that season. I was sure Eric Nesterenko wanted to pay me back for cutting his head open. Sure enough, during the warm-up he gave me a two-handed slash to the ankles, which is bad enough: you can break a guy's ankle doing that. I didn't react, though; I knew that's what he wanted. That night I kept my eye on him, but he didn't attack me again, and he didn't call me any names. Maybe he figured he didn't need me cracking my stick over his head again.

I had a chance to find out thirty years later. In 1991 I received a call from the NHL inviting me to the All-Star Game in Chicago. I was surprised—I hadn't heard from the NHL in a long time. Still, I was pleased by the invitation, so I went. The NHL put me up at the luxurious Drake Hotel and paid all the expenses for me and my wife, Deljeet.

Chicago is a really great city, with wonderful architecture, restaurants, art galleries, and people, and this time I aimed to enjoy it.

So I went to my first All-Star function, and who was there but Bobby Hull and Stan Mikita? I said hello to them both—the very guys I'd missed seeing play in my first game in Chicago, now in the same room as me. They were friendly, and Bobby still is when I see him at NHL events.

Then I walked up to the bar to get Deljeet a glass of red wine. And who was standing next to me? Eric Nesterenko. I turned to look at him, and instead of hurling a racist epithet at me or butt-ending me with a hockey stick, he said, "Hi, Willie, how's it going?"

I was stunned. After the ugly things this man had said and done to me, now he was regarding me as just another guy at the bar? Maybe he'd thought using the N-word against me was just good old-fashioned trash talking. It's not. Trash talking aims to needle an opponent by casting doubt on his strength or his intelligence or his girlfriend, but within the context of the game. Racism aims to diminish the humanity of a person, period. It's not about a game, it's about your life. There's a huge difference, as anyone who's ever been racially abused will tell you.

So I had two choices in this unexpected encounter. I could break his nose, which might be briefly satisfying but would ruin the All-Star Weekend for everyone and ensure that I never came to another one. Or I could just answer him as if meeting up was the most ordinary thing in my day. So I said, "Not too bad." Then I walked away.

His violent attack on me was something that happened a long time ago, I figured. What good would it do to bring it up now? It would have been nice to hear him say, "I'm sorry. What I said and did was wrong." I don't think I ever will.

11.

GONE

I played forty-three games for Boston during that 1960–61 season, and since a season in those days was just seventy games, I'd been up in the NHL for more than half of it. It had been a very good stretch for me, despite the ugly stuff on the ice. I could deal with that. And now that the players and fans had seen how I handled it, I figured the novelty of their bigotry would wear off.

The most important thing to me was that not only had I played those forty-plus games in the NHL, but I'd pulled them off with only one eye. My secret was still safe, and in the process I'd managed to score four goals and add ten assists for fourteen points. That wouldn't win me the NHL scoring title, but I wasn't hurting the team, either.

Still, the team had endured a pretty bad season. The Bruins were the lowest-scoring team in the NHL: we'd lost forty-two games, tied thirteen, and finished in last place with forty-three points—eleven points behind New York, who were second last. It was, in fact, the beginning of a rough patch for Boston. They would finish in last place for the next four seasons, then in second last, and then in last place again—until they put this kid named Bobby Orr on defense.

But all I knew in the summer of 1961 was that I'd be returning next season with the Bruins. I'd been invited into the office of coach Milt Schmidt and manager Lynn Patrick. Despite our last-place finish they were relaxed and friendly. Schmidt had been named to the Hockey Hall of Fame, so he was especially upbeat. "We're very impressed with your play this season," they told me. Even better, they promised me a future. "Look forward to being back with the Bruins next season," they said. "Now go home and have a great summer!"

I was so proud—and relieved, too: I'd be a Boston Bruin next season, and the season after that, and, with luck, for the rest of my NHL career. So I hustled home to Fredericton and told everyone what the Bruins had said. My parents were happy for me, my friends proud. And my brother Richard, all those years older than I, was now looking up to me. I felt like a star.

It didn't last long. I'd been home for about six weeks when a long-distance call came. My mother answered the phone and said, "Willie, it's a sportswriter from the *Telegraph-Journal* who wants to speak to you."

The *Telegraph-Journal* was Saint John, New Brunswick's big provincial paper. As I went to take the phone call, I thought that maybe finally the media was catching up with what I had accomplished, breaking the color barrier in the NHL, and then catching on in the world's best hockey league. No one had yet written such a story, and it might be time to write one now.

I picked up the phone. The sportswriter introduced himself, then asked me a stunning question.

"Willie, what do you think of the trade?"

"You have me at a disadvantage," I told him, but my heart was sinking. "I don't know what trade you mean." Why would a sportswriter be asking me about a trade unless it involved me?

The news had just come out, he explained. "You have been traded to Montreal for Cliff Pennington and Terry Gray. How do you feel about playing for the Canadiens?"

I was speechless. On the one hand, Montreal was the best team in the NHL. But on the other, Milt Schmidt and Lynn Patrick had told me, in person, that I'd be playing in Boston. The Bruins knew where I was, and yet no one had called to tell me anything about a trade.

The sportswriter was just doing his job, but he must have known how I felt: as though I'd been cracked over the head with a hockey stick. But I recovered my composure.

"If I've been traded to the Montreal Canadiens, I'll probably be playing for one of their farm teams," I told him. Montreal had won five straight Stanley Cups from 1955–56 to 1959–60. They'd finished first with ninety-two points in the 1960–61 season—almost fifty points better than the forty-three we'd earned in Boston. Montreal had brilliant players like Jean Béliveau, Henri Richard, Dickie Moore, Boom Boom Geoffrion, and a bunch more coming up in their deep farm system. I didn't think they needed me to give them that extra edge.

And yet.

I had proven myself in the NHL. I was fast and skilled and I was twenty-five years old, still young enough to get another shot at the NHL. But I wanted to know why the Bruins had done what they had done.

I waited for that call from them to explain, but no call ever came. Nor did I have a high-powered agent who could call the Bruins and demand an answer. (Actually, I didn't have one because nobody did. All of that was just beginning—and a good thing, too, since in just a few years' time, let alone today, the Bruins' treatment of me would never happen.) And it just wasn't done for a player to call management and ask hard questions. You'd be seen as a troublemaker, and that could create all kinds of professional problems. Look at what had happened to Ted Lindsay.

So I had to speculate, and to listen to other people's theories about why I was a Bruin at the end of the season and six weeks later I was not. Pennington and Gray, the guys Boston had traded me for, went on to play more than a hundred games each in the NHL. In other words, they weren't trading minor leaguers.

It came down to my blind eye, I reckon. Somehow the Bruins had found out, and instead of announcing it publicly, which would have ended my career, they just quietly dealt me to Montreal. And since they knew I'd have questions, they'd opted not to speak to me at all.

Had they known about my blind eye? Years later, Milt Schmidt said something that made me wonder. "He kept that secret as long as he could," he remarked, "because it looked to me at first as if he was just too fast for his own good. He was a good team man, but no, he couldn't have played for us if we had known he had only one eye." When I heard that, I was sure they had found out.

That said, the Bruins weren't about to get nothing in exchange for me. So although they might have privately worried about the legal consequences to them—or life consequences to me—if I were also to lose my left eye while playing for them, they certainly weren't going to let Montreal know that.

Then came a letter from Sam Pollock, manager of Montreal's farm team, the Hull-Ottawa Canadiens. Montreal had acquired my contract from Boston, he wrote, but they wanted me to report to Hull-Ottawa.

Just like that, I was back in the minor pros.

I'd taken a lot of knocks before, but this one was particularly painful. I would never have thought that my hard work and determination and perseverance against some pretty powerful odds would be undone so quickly, and so callously.

But getting stuck in my own past wasn't going to do me any good. I resolved to join the Canadiens' farm team and keep doing the thing that had gotten me into the NHL in the first place. I'd work harder than everyone else, and eventually I'd get my shot at pulling on the red, white, and blue jersey of the Montreal Canadiens. After all, they wouldn't have traded for me if they'd thought what I'd done in the NHL wasn't good enough.

In fact, going to play for the Hull-Ottawa Canadiens represented a bit of a homecoming for me. I'd played in Hull-Ottawa before. Indeed, I'd played quite well for them at the beginning of the 1960–61 season, scoring ten goals and adding nine assists in sixteen games. Until I'd gotten the call to report to the Bruins, I'd been on pace for more than a point a game.

The team practiced and played in Hull, the Quebec city that lies just across the river from Ottawa. The season before, when I was playing in Boston, the Hull-Ottawa Canadiens were the best team in the Eastern Professional Hockey League. They finished in first place, with ninety-one points, and won the league championship. It's always nice to be playing for a winner, and a large part of that was due to the brains behind the operation, Sam Pollock.

Pollock was thirty-six when I went to play for him that second time. Before he guided Hull-Ottawa to their championship he'd led the Junior Canadiens to two Memorial Cups, the Stanley Cup of junior hockey. He'd been with the Montreal Canadiens organization since he was twenty-two and would stay with them until he was fifty-three, winning nine Stanley Cups as the team's general manager.

The Montreal Canadiens have this reputation for class, poise, and success, and everyone thinks it was always thus, but back in the 1940s, the reality was anything but—especially for the city's junior teams. Not only did they play fewer games than the other junior teams, they often played late at night in the Montreal Forum, when it was hard to attract fans and even harder for players, who were fighting off sleep, to bring their A-game.

Transformation came thanks to Toronto Maple Leafs owner Conn Smythe, whose bullying finally alienated his brilliant hockey lieutenant, Frank Selke, who left Toronto in disgust and came to Montreal. From a distance it looked like a first-rate franchise, but Selke soon saw that the Canadiens, while great on the ice, had a pretty bad farm system. So he spent hundreds of thousands of dollars to build up that system and support the NHL club. At the time, Sam Pollock was the director of the Midget Canadiens—younger kids who played in the Canadiens' system. But the Junior Canadiens' coach, who was about to leave his post, told Selke that Pollock should get his job. Sam Pollock, he said, was the type of guy the Canadiens needed on their team.

Pollock was built like a bulldog and went after problems the same way. He was determined, he was great at motivating everyone else around him, and he was smart: he knew the value not just of his own players but of everyone playing in every other league.

So going to Hull-Ottawa wasn't all bad. If Sam Pollock wanted me on his team, that was saying something.

———

When I suited up for the Hull-Ottawa Canadiens at the start of the 1961–62 season, I was determined to be called up to the NHL before Christmas. But I got the call much sooner than that, and it wasn't to the NHL.

The season was only twelve games old when I showed up at the rink for a practice. It was about eight fifteen in the morning and our workout wasn't scheduled till ten, but I liked to be early. It was a way to get my gear in order and prepare to fully engage with the practice.

As soon as the team's trainer saw me he said, "Willie, Sammy wants to see you." I told him I'd see Pollock after the practice, but the trainer was firm. "No, he wants to see you right now. He's up in his office."

When a general manager wants to see a player urgently, it could mean anything—maybe I was being called up to Montreal? When I got to Pollock's office he was sitting at his desk, papers scattered all over the place. I asked him if he wanted to see me, and he said, "Yes, yes, come in."

I stood in front of his desk for a full thirty seconds as Sam sat there with his head down. He didn't look at me once. I began to fear that something bad had happened to my parents or one of my brothers or sisters. Finally, I coughed and reminded him I had a practice to get ready for. "Oh, yes, Willie," he said. "I'm glad you're here."

He stood up, walked around to the front of his desk, and put his arm around my shoulders. I noticed that he had an envelope in his hand. "Willie," he said, "from time to time the Montreal organization has to make changes in their player personnel." He smiled at me in a kind of fatherly fashion, even though he was only ten years older. "We've been impressed with your play, but we've traded you to . . ."

It was as if I were suddenly in slow motion. I'd been traded again, but I didn't want to know where, and yet I did, if it was to an NHL club. It was one of those moments where what happens next can totally change your life.

And so it did. Sam Pollock told me I'd been traded to the Los Angeles Blades of the Western Hockey League.

There was an immediate conflict in my mind as I tried to connect "hockey" with "Los Angeles." L.A. was home to the Dodgers and the Rams and the Lakers. It was hot and had palm trees and sandy beaches and no winter at all. What kind of hockey could possibly exist in Los Angeles?

I was about to find out. Pollock then handed me the envelope he'd been holding. Inside it was an airplane ticket.

"Your flight to Los Angeles leaves at twelve fifty," he said. "Today." I had just over four hours to pack up my gear, and my apartment, and my life, and catch that plane out west.

I returned to the dressing room and told the trainer the news. He was pleased for me. "You'll be having fun out there with all those movie stars," he said. I wasn't at all convinced of that as I gathered up my two pairs of skates and the couple dozen hockey sticks that I had just ordered. I hadn't even taken them out of their cellophane wrapping.

Then, back at my apartment, I got my things together. I wasn't married, didn't have a serious girlfriend, and the apartment had been rented to me fully furnished, so I had only to pack my clothes and personal items. And being a few more time zones further from my parents just meant calling them earlier in my day. It was as clean a getaway from Hull as these things can be. I went to the bank, took out some money, and then headed off to the airport to my new life.

I'd never been to the West Coast, and had certainly never imagined playing there. And now I'd have to work my way back up to the NHL from as far away from the action as one could possibly get. The closest NHL team to California was in *Chicago*, nearly two thousand miles away. In other words, I got on that plane to L.A. wondering if I'd ever be back. Part of me was excited by this West Coast adventure, and part of me was hurting at the sheer distance that would separate me from my parents and my brother. Sure, I could go back to Fredericton in the off-season; it would just be a longer plane ride. But my parents and Coot and my pals wouldn't be coming to L.A. to watch me play—and that marked the end of a ritual that had been part of my life since I played my first game.

When I'd left Hull-Ottawa it was freezing, but when I stepped out of the airplane in Los Angeles on November 12, 1961, it had to have been at least seventy-five degrees. So I took off my heavy topcoat, walked down the steps of the plane, and looked around at the palm trees rippling in the Pacific breeze under that California sunshine. I still couldn't quite grasp that hockey was played in this tropical paradise.

I caught a taxi to the Coliseum Hotel and signed in. The hotel was across the street from where the Blades played, the L.A. Memorial Sports Arena. It was new, finished in 1959—a round, very contemporary looking building, even for its day. Most, if not all, arenas I'd played in had been built like boxes, rectangular in shape, but this rink suggested the future.

As I was walking to the elevator, I noticed this guy reading a newspaper. I had only a side view of him but I knew I'd seen him before, and not in the movies. He shifted the paper and turned his head, and then I realized who it was: Jean-Marc Picard. We'd played together on the Quebec Aces in the 1956–57 season.

"Pic!" I called out.

"Hey, Willie," he said, a big smile on his face as if we'd planned to meet here. "So you've been traded, too?"

Jean-Marc, it turned out, had been traded from the San Francisco Seals to the Los Angeles Blades. We had a laugh at the coincidence. And instead of going to my room I asked the bell captain to take my gear upstairs—I was so happy to find a familiar face and to be invited out to see the sights of L.A.

That evening Jean-Marc and I wound up at a Hollywood bar, having a great time listening to Sam & Dave, who would go on to become a very popular singing group in the 1960s. I told Jean-Marc about my time playing in the NHL and he told me about his time playing in San Francisco, where he'd put in only nine games after being traded there by Winnipeg, who'd now traded him again to Los Angeles.

We had a beer or two or maybe three, and I didn't get back to my hotel room until two a.m., meaning five a.m. in Hull-Ottawa, meaning I'd been awake for nearly twenty-four hours. And during that time I'd crossed the continent and been a member of two different hockey teams.

The next morning Jean-Marc and I had a meeting at the Sports Arena. The Blades hadn't been playing there for long, having been transferred to Los Angeles the past summer from Victoria, where they'd been called the Cougars.

We were welcomed onto the team by the coach, George "Bus" Agar, a veteran of the minor leagues as both a player and coach, and given our Blades uniforms, which happened to be black and gold, just like the Boston Bruins. Then we had a practice, and that night we were playing the Calgary Stampeders.

In hockey, you may have new teammates and you may be playing in a new rink, but at least the game is the same. California and I hit it off right from the start, because in that first game I was able to score two goals. The fans cheered me on as if I'd always been there, and the papers said something like "The addition of Willie O'Ree is a good one." There's nothing like scoring a couple of goals and getting a win to make you feel at home.

Months later, in 1962, I even had a homecoming of sorts in Los Angeles when I was invited to an NAACP luncheon held to honor Jackie Robinson, who, as I have mentioned, I met back in 1949, when I was a thirteen-year-old baseball player with my heart set on hockey.

When I arrived at the luncheon with my coach and a couple of teammates, Robinson was finishing an interview with the media. So we hung back until he was done, and then went over to say hello. "Willie O'Ree!" he said, remembering me, to my great surprise. "I met you back in Brooklyn and you told me you were going to be a hockey player. And so you are."

He knew all about me. It was one of those electric moments life gives you when things come full circle in an almost magical way. There we were, together again, me and Jackie Robinson, both of us having made history.

And although Jackie Robinson was an All-Star baseball player who'd lit up major league baseball with his talent and I was a one-eyed hockey player hiding my blind eye from every league I played in just so I could keep playing, at this moment we were equals. We'd changed the sports we loved simply by being allowed to play them at the highest level. The history we made was by virtue of our athletic talent that vaulted us over the color barrier, which says a lot about how history works. Had there not been that racial barrier, there would have been no history to make. But as I stood there with Jackie Robinson, I knew we'd be joined together forever because of this history, and I could not have been prouder of what we'd done.

In my second season in L.A., my old friend Stan Maxwell came to play for the Blades. Once more we were the only two black guys and on the same team, this time in the WHL. The league was a very good one, too. The more we played, the more I loved it. For one thing, L.A. had a huge Canadian population, which fueled the demand to see hockey; we'd get eight thousand people out for a game. (In Hull-Ottawa, we'd average only two thousand.) The fans were great. And they sure knew their hockey, which, as I came to learn, had been with them for quite a while.

It was a testament to the power of the game, really, to learn how long Los Angeles had been home to hockey. The city's first game was held on February 1, 1917, at the Ice Palace, where a bunch of Canadians—no surprise—playing for the Los Angeles Athletic Club beat the University Club 7–0. The *Los Angeles Times'* report of the game let readers know that "no one was killed outright." Amateur and club hockey teams also played their games in the Palais de Glace. And by the mid-1920s hockey had made it into the universities, with USC, UCLA, and Loyola all icing teams.

Then, in April 1926, the NHL came to town when New York City's first NHL team, the New York Americans, played a series of games against an L.A. All-Star squad. A year later, the NHL's Chicago Black Hawks and Pittsburgh Pirates played games against local teams before meeting each other at the Winter Garden. The Hawks returned to L.A. in 1930 to play the Boston Bruins.

And in 1949, Frank Zamboni, who'd honed his expertise building plants for block ice, found a better way to restore arena ice at his Iceland Skating Rink in Paramount, California, just north of Long Beach, by creating the machine that's famous around the world and that bears his name.

So Los Angeles knew hockey. But the thing that really made me fall in love with L.A. was falling in love.

———

Berna Deanne Deberry was going to university in Portland, Oregon, where she was from, and so she was also a fan of the city's WHL team, the Portland Buckaroos (which I was not, but more on that later). I met her in the city when I was playing there (and where I nearly got traded until they found out about my eye). She was very attractive and very stylish. I was drawn to both—I've always liked style, and I'm not opposed to beauty, either. Berna Deanne's grandmother lived in Pasadena, so moving down to Los Angeles wasn't too much of a shock for her.

We were married in the summer of 1962, back home in Fredericton. My parents were happy about our marriage, partly because Berna Deanne was black; they thought this would give our children a clear identity and save us from bigots—well, from a strand of bigot who didn't like inter-racial marriage.

Berna Deanne wasn't too happy about my fishing adventures with Coot and Junior and Bubsy, which I managed to sneak into our honeymoon. I can imagine now how she felt spending time with her brand-new in-laws while her new husband was up at Island Lake with his pals. I think it set the tone for how she would think of her place in our marriage.

We set up house in Redondo Beach, Los Angeles, about five blocks from the water. It was paradise being so close to the Pacific—I used to go down to sit on the beach and look at the ocean and just think about the big wide world. We had great neighbors, too, friendly and diverse, so it was a fine place to start a family. And before I knew it I was a father. Our son Kevin was born in 1963, making me the happiest man on earth, followed by Darren a year later. Just like that, I'd gone from carefree hockey player to family man with two young boys and a lot of responsibility.

I'd always loved kids and had spent a lot of time in my summers back home playing sports and hanging out with them. But now that I had my own I realized that it was a 24/7, rest-of-my-life kind of job. It's not the easiest role when you're a hockey player, having to be on the road so much of the year. And with Berna Deanne looking after two young children and me married to the game from September right through to April, it put a strain on things at home.

The Blades' schedule had us traveling quite far geographically compared to the Eastern teams, who were mostly all packed together in one small region. The joke in the East was that you could play an away game and sleep in your own bed that same night. Not so out West. We'd go up the coast and then into the Canadian prairies, from San Francisco, Portland, Spokane, Seattle, and Vancouver to Calgary and Edmonton. (Then, when Calgary and Edmonton folded, Denver and Victoria came into the league.) I liked traveling the coast and was knocked out by the beauty of the West. Everywhere you looked there was some postcard picture, from the crashing surf of San Francisco to the towering fir trees of B.C. and the Rocky Mountains of Alberta. It was all gorgeous—except for Portland, Oregon, that is.

Now, I know that today Portland is one of the prettiest and most progressive cities in the United States, but I hated playing there, even though it's where I met my wife. First off, the Buckaroos played in a rink that was smaller than NHL regulation (which is 200 feet long by 85 feet wide). Today NHL rinks are all the same size, but back then they varied. Portland's rink was just 185 feet long and maybe 80 feet wide—and they used it to their advantage. For example, the Portland guys knew exactly how long it took the puck to get around the boards. Those of us used to the bigger rink thought it would take a second or two longer, so we'd be a step late. Then the Portland guys would run us into the boards hard. The blue lines were closer to center ice as well, which could mess with your timing; thanks to the shortened rink, you'd suddenly find yourself offside.

But those things were just part of hockey in Portland back then, and I could deal with it. What I hated about the place was having to play against a Portland Buckaroo named Doug Messier.

He'd always hit me from behind or spear me, and just like Eric Nesterenko, he'd use racial slurs against me, the N-word being his favorite. And yet when I'd heard enough and challenged him to show me just how superior he was, he'd never drop his gloves and fight me like a man. As a hockey guy, especially back then, you're expected to back up your words and your actions. If you take a cheap shot, you have to pay your bill. If you say something the other guy doesn't like, you're going to be held to account. People may not like it, but that's actually something that keeps players honest, and polite. So acting out *and* refusing to pay your bill—no one respects a player like that.

In short, Messier and I did not like each other. When he refused to back up his words I figured I had to use my stick against him. We had terrible stick fights because he was such a coward. The guy's son turned out to be one of the greatest NHL players ever, but this is one instance where "like father, like son" doesn't apply.

In my first season with Los Angeles—still playing left wing, still with a blind right eye—I scored twenty-eight goals and added twenty-six assists. In my next season I scored twenty-five and helped on twenty-six others. These numbers were some of my best ever, but things were going to get even better.

It was at the start of the 1963–64 season, my third in L.A., that Alf Pike came to coach the Blades. Pike not only had an excellent hockey pedigree; he was also a great coach. And he changed my game forever.

Pike came from Winnipeg—he'd gone to a hockey school there run by Lester Patrick (father of Lynn in Boston), one of the greatest hockey men ever, who was then coaching the New York Rangers. Patrick signed Pike as a nineteen-year-old to play with the Rangers' farm team. By 1940 Pike had moved up to the NHL: he was the Rangers' twenty-two-year-old rookie center who scored a big goal against Toronto to win the 1940 Stanley Cup.

It was Pike, nicknamed "The Embalmer" for working at a funeral home in the off-season, who singlehandedly shot a major dose of life back into my game. With seven left-wingers in Los Angeles and not enough right-wingers, he put me on right wing. Suddenly my good left eye was on the same side as the play and my blind right eye on the side of the boards as I skated down the right wing. I'd never thought of doing that. And yet, once Alf made the suggestion, it seemed an act of genius. And it changed my hockey life.

By the end of that 1964–65 season I'd scored thirty-eight goals and added twenty-one assists, my highest goal total since I'd been a pro hockey player. And I won the WHL scoring title—the first time I'd won a scoring title as a pro, and with one blind eye. (If I'd switched to right wing in Boston, would I have stayed with the team?) So now, in the summer of 1966, I was daring to hope that my newfound touch on the ice might get me another shot at the NHL.

There was another reason for hope: the NHL had decided to give Los Angeles a franchise when the league expanded in 1967. And there I was already, an NHL veteran and the leading scorer on the L.A. Blades. It looked like the Montreal Canadiens had done me a huge favor in sending me west. I'd once thought I'd gone as far away from the NHL as a man could get—but now that it was coming right to my own backyard, I knew I'd have another chance to play in the greatest hockey league on earth.

12.

A GULL IN SAN DIEGO

In the summer of 1967 the United States was in tumult. Ten years earlier, when I went to Georgia to try out for baseball's Milwaukee Braves, I'd experienced firsthand the ugliness of the Jim Crow South and had seen how starkly racist America remained. In the decade since then much had changed, and much was still changing, some for better, some for worse. But it felt at times as if my adopted country was about to explode.

The U.S. was at war in Vietnam, and in 1967 public opinion against that war was growing loud and strong, with marches taking place across the country. But it was more than marching—it was a feeling that the war was wrong, and way too costly in lives lost. Every night on the evening news we'd see the casualty numbers: young Americans killed in battle so far from home and for reasons no one could quite explain.

There was a war at home as well—one that directly affected me. In 1964 the U.S. government under President Lyndon Johnson had finally passed the Civil Rights Act, making any kind of discrimination or segregation based on race illegal. But reality hadn't caught up with the ideal. People, African American people, were still very much discriminated against by white society. And while Los Angeles wasn't the Deep South, it had serious issues.

To be a professional hockey player in Los Angeles was unusual in itself back then, but as a black man I was part of a rising black population that had come to the city during the Second World War in what was known as the Second Great Migration. President Roosevelt had signed an executive order prohibiting defense companies, many based in Los Angeles, from discriminating on the basis of race, and so black people headed for Southern California to take up this opportunity. But despite laws and good intentions, the reality in Los Angeles was that black people couldn't live in white neighborhoods, even after the Civil Rights Act was passed. So there were overwhelmingly black L.A. neighborhoods like Watts, which was about thirteen miles south of downtown and eighteen miles east of the Pacific. And it was in Watts where terrible rioting had erupted in the summer of 1965.

The inciting incident was all too familiar: a white cop stopped a black motorist, and things quickly got out of hand. The driver was arrested for being drunk. His mother, angry at her son, blew up. Then she went after the police, who arrested them both. Word got out that a black woman had been roughed up by white cops, and it all went badly downhill from there.

After six days of rioting, thirty-four people—twenty-five of them black—were dead and more than a thousand were injured. At least six hundred buildings had been damaged or destroyed by fire and looting, most of them white-owned. Firefighters who tried to put out the fires were shot at by snipers. Eventually the National Guard was brought in to restore order. Armed soldiers patrolled the streets and erected blockades, warning that anyone who tried to pass through them would be shot, no questions asked. In a matter of days we'd gone from being a free-spirited city to a tense, occupied battleground.

I noticed people looking at me differently. I was a Canadian hockey player living in L.A., but unless you saw me on the ice, all you saw was another black man who might be thinking of overthrowing the white power structure. It was a strange feeling, and it made me uncomfortable while it lasted—which, in many ways, you could say it still does. I mean, I still get people judging me because of my color. That's the tragedy of us-versus-them thinking. People thought they knew me because of what I looked like. Sure, not many black men in Los Angeles are Canadian hockey players. But if the way you think makes you blind to the presence of someone like me when I'm on the sidewalk right beside you, then you're missing out. That's true for anyone who thinks they know another before they take the time to understand them.

The damage to L.A. was terrible and long-lasting. The fact that today the week of death and destruction Los Angeles suffered is also known as the Watts Rebellion underlines the conflict between black people and white in America at the time.

And I actually saw that damage myself. My Los Angeles Blades teammate Warren Hynes worked off-season for a business that had customers in Watts, and he needed to meet with them. The prospect scared him, though, so he asked me to go along, and I did.

When we drove into Watts it was like driving into a war zone. And with soldiers on the streets looking at everything and everyone as a potential problem, we tried to seem harmless, which was hard to do at a time like that. I saw burned-out buildings and people who looked like me in a state of rage and despair. But despite the tension and the sorrow, we didn't encounter any trouble, although we did get a couple of surprised looks—people must have wondered what this black man was doing in the neighborhood with a white guy.

In the end Warren met with his customers and we drove back out. It had been surreal to see up close what I'd been seeing only on the television news, and it stayed with me. This was part of the city where I'd never lived myself, but now that I'd inhaled its air I could feel the anger that had sparked the rioting. I'm not saying that rioting is the right response—I'm just saying that I got the anger. And I understood that if justice isn't done, that anger will do damage.

By then, with a two-year-old and a newborn, Berna Deanne wondered if we should return to Canada. But I was committed to my career in Los Angeles, and we weren't living in Watts. So we stayed, hoping that the riots would mark the beginning of social change.

Not long after that, Dr. Martin Luther King came to Los Angeles. And although he strongly condemned the violence and destruction that had been unleashed upon the city, his views on the event spoke powerfully to me. The cause of the riot, King said, was "environmental and not racial. The economic deprivation, social isolation, inadequate housing, and general despair of thousands of Negroes teeming in Northern and Western ghettos are the ready seeds which give birth to tragic expressions of violence."

King went on to say that, until everyone was treated with dignity, and until equality and justice ruled the land, these flashpoints were still in danger of exploding, especially since some black leaders believed that the only way to get white America to notice the inequality and injustice was to burn things down.

Those flashpoints went off again in that summer of 1967, when the NHL was about to come to Los Angeles. Race riots began in Buffalo in June. Then, in July, race riots flared in Minneapolis, Newark, Milwaukee, and Detroit. In August they lit up Washington, D.C. Many people were killed, and many inner-city neighborhoods and businesses were destroyed.

I would also like to note that, in the middle of all that destruction and violence, something good happened in that August of 1967: Thurgood Marshall was confirmed as the first African American justice of the U.S. Supreme Court. It had been a long time coming, but perhaps it was a sign that this cauldron in which we were living would produce real and lasting change.

As a black Canadian living in the United States, I was in the middle of it all. I wasn't political, and I hadn't grown up with the same kind of discrimination these rioters were violently opposing, but my very color put me on one side of the battle. To be sure, as I played the game I loved so much I'd always had to fight a silent battle against those who thought my color was somehow a problem. I'd since made it to the NHL. My color was no longer an issue for me. But everywhere I turned it was the dominant issue of the day. More than ever now I was a "black" hockey player in the States, with all the political baggage that entailed, when all I wanted to do was win another scoring title and a league championship. In the NHL. And whenever anyone mentioned that I was the first African American to play in the NHL, I would gently remind them that I was a Canadian, of African ancestry.

I had never defined my game by my color, but only by how I played it. And yet, just as leaving home for the American South had taught me a great deal about racism, my life in Los Angeles was showing me a subtler, creeping kind of racism that isn't necessarily degrading or deliberately insulting. It may even be friendly in its own way, I suppose. But it's still a constraint on freedom. Unlike others who came before me, I was allowed to play hockey. But I wasn't allowed to *only* play hockey. That was impossible. I was always seen as a black player before I was seen as a hockey player. I would never complain. Part of being first means going through difficulties. I accept that. And I know that even today, black NHLers are never *just* hockey players.

What I want for young people today is what I wanted for myself back then. I was looking forward to the upcoming season, just like other players. There was big excitement about the Kings coming to L.A., and I was as eager for the big time as anyone else.

Oddly enough, it was my old Hull-Ottawa general manager, Sam Pollock, who had a hand in the NHL coming to Southern California. Sam had moved up to the Canadiens in 1964—and his hockey smarts weren't lost on the NHL, who asked him to head up a committee looking at putting a few new teams into the NHL mix.

Now, this was an exciting time for pro sports in the States. Television had discovered just how profitable it could be, and as a result TV networks were giving fat contracts to pro sports leagues. Two years before, in 1965, NBC had paid more than $30 million for TV rights to Major League Baseball—and the NHL wanted some of that money. In order to get it, though, they needed teams in American markets that would attract American viewers and TV network attention.

So Sam Pollock and his committee recommended that the NHL expand from the so-called Original Six to a twelve-team NHL, with a whole new division created from the new teams in Minnesota, Pittsburgh, Philadelphia, St. Louis, Oakland, and Los Angeles. (To show you the power of the money, Vancouver had been promised a franchise in the expansion, but the ownership in Toronto and Montreal didn't want to divvy up TV revenues three ways. So much for

Canada's game when it came to profits.)

Blades owner Dan Reeves had taken a shot at becoming the NHL's L.A. franchise, but he had company: Los Angeles Lakers owner Jack Kent Cooke, a transplanted Canadian like me; Buffalo Bills owner Ralph Wilson; TV producer Tony Owen, who'd created *The Donna Reed Show* and had been a vice-president of the Detroit Lions football team; and a media group called Metromedia.

The Blades were considered the favorites. Not only had we been playing pro hockey in the city since 1961, we also had our own Sports Arena (or rather, we were the first choice of the city's Coliseum Commission, who owned the arena). And an ace card seemed to be that our owner, Dan Reeves, also co-owned the Los Angeles Rams, so his sporting footprint was significant. And since the NHL had promised the Blades NHL expansion rights, Reeves was going to do a very American thing and sue them if the Blades didn't get the franchise.

Jack Kent Cooke, meanwhile, told the NHL that if he got the franchise he'd build a larger, brand-new arena out of his own pocket. Cities always love to hear from deep-pocketed people who'll build shiny new arenas at their own expense, but no one thought he could do it—a new arena cost a lot of money, and he didn't have a lot of time.

But then, neither did we. If we didn't change our fortunes in the 1966–67 season and show the NHL that we were L.A.'s hockey club, our chances of landing the franchise were slim. In the two previous seasons we'd finished bottom of the league. Attendance was down as well. But I'd given my best, as I always did—thirty-four goals, twenty-six assists—and it had helped the Blades finish second from last in the WHL that season.

When the NHL awarded the new L.A. franchise to Jack Kent Cooke, who was building his new arena for $16 million in Inglewood, the game was over for the Blades. With the new Los Angeles Kings not wanting to compete with another pro team in the city, we played our last game in April 1967.

The other blow to me was the nature of the June 1967 NHL expansion draft. It allowed the new teams to take twenty players each from the existing Original Six, who could also put their best players on a "protected list," meaning they were excluded from the draft. Also on that protected list were junior players, and any player who'd been sold to the Western Hockey League before June 1966. And that meant me.

So in the summer of 1967 I waited for a phone call or a letter inviting me to play for another team. I just knew it wasn't going to be an NHL team.

Finally, the phone rang. On the other end was Max McNab, general manager of the San Diego Gulls. The Gulls, who'd come into the Western Hockey League in the 1966–67 season, hadn't done very well, finishing just after us, in last place. They needed help.

In the late 1940s Max had played three seasons for the Detroit Red Wings on teams boasting such talents as Gordie Howe, Ted Lindsay, and Red Kelly. He was a six-foot-two, left-hand-shooting centerman whose NHL career had been cut short because of back surgery. He'd since turned to coaching and had joined the Gulls in the previous season.

And now Max McNab was asking me what I was going to do about my career.

"Willie," he said, "are you planning on playing hockey this year?"

I was now thirty-two, and to tell you the truth, I didn't know. Max said he'd help me make a decision. He wanted me to play for him.

I was in a pretty grim place that summer. My marriage had broken up the year before, and Berna Deanne was gone. She'd seen my long absences as a statement of my attitude toward family life and I'd seen them as doing my job to provide food and shelter for my family, but it was clear she was never going to accept that. Nor was I going to give up hockey. I mean, it was my life, and my family was my family. But Berna Deanne thought hockey was more important to me, and I could not convince her otherwise.

So she left, taking my sons with her, to live in Portland. Kevin and Darren, even though they were still little guys, hadn't yet shown any interest in hockey. I'd been looking forward to teaching them the game I loved, but I didn't see them very much except when we played in Portland, which wasn't often enough. It was tough.

Over the years to come Berna Deanne moved around a lot, which meant it was difficult to keep up with the boys. They'd started playing hockey after they moved away from me, and played until they were fifteen or sixteen. I told them, "Don't

think that because your name is O'Ree it's going to be easy."
I didn't mean that ironically, either. I was proud of what I'd
accomplished, but they were on their own, and it's one of my
regrets that we were separated for so long. It's a hard thing to
recover from, lost time, and I've done better at it with Kevin
than with Darren.

All of which is to say that when Max McNab called me,
I was single again and free to pick up and move to any team
that wanted me, just as I'd done when I got traded to L.A. six
years earlier. I loved living in Southern California, where I
could play a winter game in endless summer, and playing San
Diego would allow me to remain there. Also, by now I'd put
in six good seasons with Los Angeles. Maybe it was time for a
change of cities to help me move forward with my life.

So I drove down to San Diego, which is about a three-hour
trip from L.A., almost as far as the Mexican border. I used
to think it strange to be playing hockey in Los Angeles, but
playing in Mexico's backyard? Could hockey even exist there?

The first thing I did was meet with Max McNab, who
struck me as a good guy. He even had a Maritime connection:
McNab's Island in Nova Scotia is named after his family, who
settled there in the late eighteenth century, about the same
time as my ancestor Paris O'Ree was making his way to freedom in New Brunswick.

I liked San Diego as well. It was a much smaller city than
Los Angeles, with just over 600,000 people (it's more than
doubled since) and an even better climate, since it doesn't get
as scorching in the summer. Mild winters, warm summers,
and a very easy place on the eyes, with the Pacific breeze

keeping the palm trees swaying and generating some serious surf if you like to ride the waves. (I prefer to fish in the water, not surf on it.)

When the Spanish settled in California in the eighteenth century, San Diego was their first encampment, and so there's a Spanish feel to its architecture and a Mexican feel to its city life. This isn't surprising, of course, since Mexico is about a fifteen-minute drive south. (And I'm happy to report that today Mexico has a national ice hockey team and is a member of the International Ice Hockey Federation—which again proves my point that hockey is for everyone.)

So now I had a decision to make. By that time I'd been away from Canada for six years, and I had the feeling that if I stayed in the U.S., I might be there for a long time. I was still going home after the season, spending the summers fishing and hanging out with Coot and my friends. And when I lived in L.A. my mom would come and visit; she liked it for the weather and the beach, but mainly because I was playing there. My dad, though, had never come to see me out west, always saying, "Let your mom go." Of the two, she was the traveler.

But if I wanted to keep playing, I had to stay where I was wanted. I had a few good years of pro hockey still in me, and deep down I still hoped that an NHL expansion team might call me up for my experience and my ability to score, now that I'd switched wings and could see so much more of the ice.

So I signed with the Gulls, as did my old center iceman

from L.A., Warren Hynes. We picked up where we'd left off. I was still playing right wing and having a great time on the ice. In my first three seasons with the Gulls, I scored eighty-three goals and helped on ninety-six others. I won the scoring title again in 1968–69, with another thirty-eight-goal season and forty-one assists. I was as good as I'd ever been. And the NHL went on without me.

There was even more NHL expansion, with a team finally in Vancouver and another in Buffalo in 1970, but by then I knew I wouldn't make it back in. I have no idea how they found out, but the NHL had learned about my blind right eye and had underlined their rule that forbade anyone who was blind in one eye from playing in the league. I'd be playing the rest of my professional career in the WHL, which was fine with me.

I made guest appearances at sports dinners and on radio shows in San Diego. I was paid well for what I was doing, and I loved hockey more than ever. I had done what I said I would do, and had made this wonderful game my professional career.

Hockey had taken me all across this great continent of North America, but after a couple of seasons with the Gulls, I finally felt I had found my home. I loved the city, and was a star on the Gulls—not because I was a black player, but because I could play hockey at a pretty fine level. And I was going to keep playing for as long as I could.

13.

ALL GOOD THINGS . . .

There's an expression in hockey that translates out in the wider world because of its plain poetry: "hanging up your skates." It means retiring, and while some people are lucky to have jobs they love waking up to until their last breath on earth, being a professional athlete isn't one of them.

I'd kept myself in great shape, and still do, but after playing a demanding sport at the highest levels for such a long time, eventually there comes a day when you're no longer your fastest, or your best.

I played for the San Diego Gulls until the end of the 1973–74 season. I was nearly forty years old, and had played hockey for a long time—since I was five. I'd had some wonderful teammates, I'd played in the NHL, and I'd seen so many great places and met such fine people that I considered myself as having had a very good career. But every hockey player dreads the day you know is coming: the day when you have to hang up your skates, the day when you say goodbye to the game that has been your life.

A few things helped me decide that the time to hang them up was right. One of them was love. I'd been divorced for a few years and hadn't really been serious about anyone since. Little did I know, but that was about to change—and again because of hockey.

When I was on the road with the Gulls in Victoria, British Columbia, I met a beautiful Indo-Canadian woman, named Deljeet, who worked for the Hudson's Bay Company. I didn't meet her in that famous Canadian department store, though. A guy who was writing about hockey in Victoria invited me to dinner with her, as she was a fan. She had three hockey-nut brothers, so it went with the family territory, but she also really loved the game and was knowledgeable about it. I was impressed. We got to talking, and found that we had a lot in common. After that we spoke on the phone a lot. A bit later she drove down to San Diego with a couple of her friends; I got them tickets to the game. And pretty soon we fell in love.

In one of those unexpected ironies, her parents were against our relationship—not because I was black but because I wasn't Indian. If Deljeet married me, she'd be marrying outside her race. But the 1960s had done so much to change cultural boundaries that interracial marriage had become much less of a threat to society than it had been a decade earlier. In fact, at the 1968 Academy Awards, *Guess Who's Coming to Dinner*—about a white woman bringing her black fiancé home to meet her liberal parents—won two Oscars and was nominated for several more. Interracial marriage had become part of the cultural mainstream.

But I was getting married not because Hollywood said it was okay, but because I was in love. So, on November 6, 1969, Deljeet and I joined that cultural mainstream when we got married in a small church in San Diego. My teammates Warren Hynes, Freddy Hilts, and Bobby Champoux were in attendance, but no one from Fredericton or from Deljeet's family. After the wedding we went to visit Deljeet's parents in Duncan, B.C., and it was then that they accepted me. So did her uncles and cousins and nephews and nieces. They knew of my career and were hockey fans, but they soon became Willie fans, too.

A few years after that, in 1972, I had a bit of a personality clash with Jack Evans, the Gulls coach, with the result that although I still practiced with the team—I mean, I was still officially a Gull—I was no longer actually playing for them. That's when Parker McDonald came to the rescue. Parker had had a long NHL career; I'd played against him back in the 1960–61 season when he was a left-winger for the Detroit Red Wings. And now, as coach of the American Hockey League's New Haven Nighthawks, he invited me to come join the team for part of the 1972–73 season.

I was happy living in San Diego but feeling sour about the Gulls, so I didn't object too much to disrupting our life in California to go and play in Connecticut. At least I'd be playing hockey.

The Nighthawks had just entered the AHL and were an NHL affiliate as well, with connections to the Minnesota North Stars and the New York Islanders. But as I said, the NHL was done with me because of my eye, so I went to New Haven with no objective other than to do my best for the team.

New Haven is an interesting place, to put it mildly. It's home to Yale, one of the world's great universities, and so there are museums and galleries and libraries and bookshops and restaurants that go with this great institution. But the city was also home to poverty and blight and crime waves, made stark by the grandness of the university. It was a long way from San Diego in many ways. Still, I resolved to play my game, put in my time, and then, with any luck, return to the Gulls without any trouble. But trouble came right at the start, when I tried to rent a place for us to live.

I called the rental agent, told her my name and that I'd be playing for the New Haven hockey club, and said I'd like to rent her lakeside cottage—that it reminded me of my trips to Island Lake in New Brunswick. It was pretty and peaceful, and I love being near the water. When the agent said she'd need a deposit, I told her I'd be happy to deliver it that afternoon at the cottage. I got there early and saw her car pull up. When she started to walk toward me, I got out of my car—and when she saw me she slowed down. I knew exactly what was going to happen. She gave me a fake smile and said,

"Oh, Mr. O'Ree, I tried to call you earlier. The cottage has been rented." She was lying through her teeth.

By that point in my life I could tell in a heartbeat when someone was a racist. Already I wanted to get out of Connecticut—and sure enough, the theme that had raised its ugly head at that cottage by the lake continued in the American Hockey League.

Now, I'd been called nasty names in the Western Hockey League. And in some places fans had booed me—whether that was because I was black or maybe because I was scoring on their goalies. A couple of times I got into it when I was in the penalty box: if fans were particularly obnoxious I'd shout back at them, and on a couple of occasions, after some idiot had spat on me, I even went up into the stands (security quickly got between us and took the offender away before it got ugly). But on the whole, it wasn't too bad.

When I joined the AHL, though, some of the teams we played were in the South, a place I had no desire to visit again after my time in Waycross, Georgia. But now I was playing hockey games in Virginia, which, of course, had two teams in the league.

When we'd play in Virginia, fans—or so-called fans—would yell at me, "Why aren't you out pickin' cotton?" They'd shout out the N-word, too. But the worst thing they did was something that even now takes my breath away in its cruelty.

They threw a live black cat out onto the ice while I was playing. Just consider the effort that must have gone into that insane act: you'd have to smuggle a live cat from wherever into a noisy, crowded hockey arena, keep it under wraps until you saw me on the ice, and then throw that terrified animal with sufficient force so that it would clear the glass barrier and land on the ice. It's so crazy on so many levels that it boggles the mind.

That poor cat used up one of its nine lives when it landed. It must have been as stunned as I was because it didn't move as I skated over, picked it up, and gave it to the trainer, the fans shouting and name-calling all the while. All I can say is that the cat and I were both happy to get out of that rink (although the cat was still stuck in Virginia with those redneck racists).

I had another bad experience, this time while playing against the Clippers in Baltimore. We'd won our game—which was rare in that season; out of seventy-six games we ended up winning only sixteen—so a bunch of us went out for dinner to celebrate. Baltimore is famous for its seafood, and we were going to enjoy the cuisine of Charm City.

A couple of the New Haven players were already in the restaurant when the rest of us arrived. But when the doorman, who was supposed to welcome guests, saw me he wouldn't let me in. "No blacks allowed" is what he said. I couldn't believe what I was hearing. It was now 1973 and we had moved on, or so I thought. But it was clear that, in the United States, if you lived south of a certain line of latitude and east of a certain line of longitude, you'd meet people stuck in the nineteenth century.

The players with me, all Canadian guys, looked at this doorman as if he were from another planet. But he refused to budge. So one of the guys went into the restaurant, got the other players out, and we all ate somewhere more civilized that night.

I stayed with the Nighthawks for fifty games, contributing twenty-one goals and twenty-four assists. But I was very happy to return to the Gulls: they were aiming to make the playoffs, Jack Evans needed me, and they called me back. So I got the last word.

I closed out the season with another six goals and five assists in eighteen games. We made the playoffs that year, taking on the Phoenix Roadrunners in the first round of a best-of-seven series. The Roadrunners won in six games before going on to win the league championship. I hate losing, but it stings a little less when the team that beats you is the best in the league.

We played them again in the playoffs the following season, when I scored thirty goals (in the process racking up my highest penalty total ever, eighty-nine minutes). This time the Roadrunners beat us in four games straight.

One of my favorite games in that 1973–74 season came on January 3, 1974, when we took on the Russian national team before a standing-room-only crowd of 13,431—the largest in our past three seasons and the fourth largest in San Diego's hockey history.

The Russians had come to town the year before (when I was with New Haven) and beat us 8–2. Still, I was excited about getting in this game, particularly since the Russians had nearly beaten Team Canada—a team of star NHL players—in an eight-game series in 1972. Everyone wanted to take their measure.

Well, they certainly gave it to us, winning 11–3. I was astonished by their speed and skill. I mean, in my younger days I was maybe the fastest player in every league I played in. But the Russians kicked it all up a notch. In fact, they were so talented that they didn't need to use their excellent goalie Vladislav Tretiak that night, nor their skilled and elegant forward Valeri Kharlamov. I was impressed by how good they were and by how they changed the game.

I was also happy just to be able to skate with them. For one thing, the language barrier meant there was no trash talk. They played a clean game, too—it was great hockey. And although the fans hated them—the Cold War was still going on, America and the U.S.S.R. staring each other down on the global stage—out there on the ice we were all just hockey players playing the game we all loved. You know I hate losing, but just seeing how good those guys were up close made playing against them a lot of fun.

At the end of the 1973–74 season, the Gulls folded. It wasn't exactly news to us. In May the owner of our arena had told us to get out by the end of the month in order to make way for the New Jersey Knights, who were relocating to San Diego as the Mariners.

The team was part of the World Hockey Association, an upstart professional league that was challenging the NHL. So, in an attempt to ward them off, the NHL granted two expansion franchises for the 1975–76 season. The Gulls president, Bob Breitbard, had tried to get one of these but was blocked by the fact that the Mariners' contract with the Sports Arena left no room for playing dates.

The NHL chose Seattle and Denver as their expansion franchises. But they didn't then put teams in either city—so you have to wonder whether they'd just been bluffing as a countermove against the WHA. In fact, neither city would really join the league for years—Denver in 1995 when the Quebec Nordiques relocated there, and Seattle, which will begin play in 2021.

So in June 1974, with no arena to play in and the WHA making incursions into the hockey market in the west, the Western Hockey League officially folded and the Gulls and Roadrunners shut down.

I moved on to the San Diego Sharks, who were part of the Pacific Southwest Hockey League. The PSHL, a semiprofessional league, operated in California, Nevada, and Alaska from 1972 through 1995. A PSHL season was short, ranging from fifteen to thirty games between anywhere from four to eight teams. I guess I can trace the trajectory of my career up and down, from my climb to the Bruins to my games in this particular loop.

It was pretty much like a circus, that league. Fighting played a big role in the action. And as part of the teams' marketing efforts, PSHL games were often paired with side attractions like broomball and roller derby. It was not for hockey purists.

I gave them two seasons, and then I retired. I wanted to spend more time with Deljeet, who was working in the financial aid office at the University of San Diego, and I was tired of all the travel. Until you play in a western league—with its greater distances between league cities—you don't realize how much travel you have to do. So whenever I hear a player on a western team mention this, I know it's not just an excuse but a genuine source of fatigue. Travel takes a lot out of you, or rather, what's left after you've given it your all on the ice.

There really is no such thing as a retired hockey player. There are just guys who don't play hockey anymore.

I'd been a professional hockey player my entire adult life, and then suddenly I wasn't. That is, I wasn't playing. But every instinct I'd built up over a long career told me it was time to go to the rink every afternoon. I still had the competitive juices, still wanted to be with the guys. It's a reality that every pro athlete has to deal with: the silence and loneliness and feelings of loss that come when you're no longer part of a team, playing the game that has defined your life.

But I've never been one to dwell on problems; I've always tried to find my solution. I'm not criticizing those who are built differently, but forward motion has always been my default direction—and now that I wasn't a hockey player I needed to find something else to do.

My goal was to get back into hockey—somehow, any way I could—but I was a long way from the ice. I worked in construction, I worked for Pepsi driving a truck, I was the assistant manager of three Jack in the Box restaurants, and I sold cars at John Hine Pontiac in the Mission Valley in San Diego. I was pretty good at it, as I like people, and of course my fame as a hockey player drew in customers. But I was still restless.

When you've spent twenty-one years as a professional athlete, when you've heard the roar of the crowd and felt the thrill of scoring a goal, any goal, it can seem as if your life has suddenly been switched to slow motion when you leave the arena for civilian street. But I knew my playing days were over, and that this was something I was going to have to process. I also knew that it wasn't the excitement I craved so much as the competition. To put it another way, I missed testing myself. So I figured I'd just have to do that with whatever team I would find myself on.

Then came the prospect of entering the security business. A guy named Mike Gore, whose dad was San Diego's chief of police, ran Strategic Security and invited me to join the company. I was reluctant at first, since I didn't know a thing about security. But Mike said I had only to take a test to get a California state "guard card." Security, he added, would be a piece of cake for me—especially after so long watching out for myself on the ice, and through one eye to boot. I was happy selling cars, though, so I thanked him for the offer and wished him luck. Then, six months later, Mike called me again to say that a position had come open. And now I wanted to give it a try.

So I set about getting a guard card. In California, the state's Bureau of Security and Investigative Services requires you to go through training before you can get a license to become a registered security guard. First I had to do eight hours of instruction in the Powers to Arrest, then another forty hours of courses that covered all kinds of things, such as state law, patrol techniques, report writing, how to question people, and so on. I got my guard card, and I was even licensed to carry a "concealed weapon," which means a gun you wear under your suit jacket. It was strange to be wearing a gun on the job. And I'm happy to say that, in the fifteen years I would spend in security, I never once had to use it.

At first my job was to go around to the various stores and construction sites that had our security guards on-site and check up on them. I was working the night shift, so I'd often find guards asleep on the job—which wasn't surprising, since unless you get trouble, the night shift can be long and dull. I was sympathetic to the guys and didn't want anyone to lose their job for nodding off at three a.m. in the dead quiet, so I'd just give them a warning and move on. I mean, you look out for your teammates.

Eventually I moved to the day shift—and, as it happened, found myself back in the world of pro sports. Strategic Security looked after security for the National Football League's San Diego Chargers. Working Chargers' games, I figured, would be a kind of career extension for me: if I wasn't going to be a professional athlete, at least I'd be around them, and who knows where that could lead? I was writing a new chapter of my life, and while my aim was to somehow get back into hockey, I'd go where the story took me. And the NFL was a pretty good place to be.

Security for an NFL game is a huge operation. I'd leave our house in Santee, a suburb of San Diego, early on game day—which, unless we were in the playoffs or on *Monday Night Football*, was always Sunday—and make the twenty-minute drive to San Diego Stadium out in Mission Valley East. I was used to playing in hockey rinks that could hold fifteen thousand people or so, but that stadium could hold *seventy* thousand, which presented that many more challenges in keeping everyone safe. I really enjoyed it, too. This was the kind of competition that mattered. Me against the bad guys.

By this time I was the security supervisor, meaning I'd sit up in the command post with the fire marshal and police officers. We would watch the crowd on video screens and through binoculars and check in with each other on walkie-talkies. We also got to see the game, which was a bonus. Dan Fouts had just joined the Chargers as quarterback, so I was able to see him at the beginning of his Hall of Fame career.

There were never any real problems at Chargers games, just rowdy drunks acting up sometimes and people trying to smuggle in marijuana and other drugs. Neither were there master terrorist plots, as in the 1977 movie *Black Sunday*, where bad guys try to blow up the Super Bowl. Still, those NFL Sundays were long, what with the pre-game planning, working the game itself, then the post-game debriefing. It was a good twelve-hour day, just as it had been when I played on the ice. Which I still dreamed about doing—I missed the game something fierce. I knew my playing days were done, but somehow, somewhere, I wanted to get back into hockey.

—

I liked working security, but when Strategic underwent cutbacks I moved on to a job at the Hotel del Coronado, on San Diego's Coronado Island. "The Del," as it's called, is one of the most spectacular hotels in the world—a huge white Spanish-style building right on the edge of the Pacific Ocean, with white sandy beaches and tennis courts, swimming pools, massive outdoor patios, and wonderful gardens filled with all kinds of tropical plants and flowers. It's the most famous building in San Diego. So you could say that I was once again in the big leagues, even though still far from the ice.

Inside, the Del has beautiful wood paneling everywhere, and fine restaurants and bars, and first-rate shops. It's a very elegant place. We'd get lots of weddings and big fancy parties there, with lots of folks just passing through to take a look— although some of them were up to doing more than that, which is where I came in. I'd walk between eight and eleven miles a day, keeping track of the action, and keeping myself in shape for whatever was coming next.

The Del has seen a lot of famous people visit since it was built in the 1880s; it's still one of California's largest all-wood structures. When it opened in 1888 it was the largest resort hotel in the world, and the first to use electrical lighting. Thomas Edison, the genius inventor, installed the electric lights himself. L. Frank Baum, author of *The Wonderful Wizard of Oz*, stayed in the hotel while he wrote the book. Some people even think the turrets in Emerald City were inspired by those on top of the hotel. I found myself wondering whether any of its guests inspired other characters, because I can tell you, the entire world passed through the Del.

It's a place everyone wants to see, and a lot of people have seen it on the silver screen, since a number of movies have been filmed there, my favorite being *Some Like It Hot*. The one everyone wants to know about, though, is *1408*, the movie based on the Stephen King story about a haunted hotel room—a room that was inspired by the Del.

King called his story "1408" because the room's numbers add up to unlucky thirteen, but the room that actually inspired him is number 3502. It's been investigated by ghost hunters, one of whom found thirty-seven "abnormalities," among them changes in temperature, magnetic fields, and electronic emissions with no observable cause. Phantoms have been reported prowling the hallways and going up and down the stairs, although I never saw any, and toilets were said to flush by themselves and so on, but my job was to keep watch on things I could see, and ghosts weren't one of them.

Even though I enjoyed my work—and was good at it, being named Employee of the Year twice—I still wanted to get back into hockey. Just one more time.

And so I did. In 1978–79 I played fifty-three games for the Pacific Hockey League's San Diego Hawks. I'm pleased to say that my forty-three-year-old self scored twenty-one goals and added twenty-five assists. (The league leader, Jerry Holland of the Spokane Flyers, scored thirty-eight goals, and he was twenty-four at the time.)

And then I quit hockey for good. Deljeet was pregnant; I was going to be a father again. Our daughter, Chandra, was born in July 1979. And this time I vowed that, instead of chasing pucks up and down the coast, I was going to be home for the baby.

In the winter of that year, my father, Harry, died at the age of eighty-eight. The ground was still too hard to dig his grave, so we waited until summer to bury him. My father had had a good long life, and had seen much change for the good. And although I didn't give a eulogy at his funeral, if I had I would have thanked him for being a great father to me and my brothers and sisters, and for supporting us all as we made our way in a world that was better because of him. I was happy that he'd lived to see me achieve my dream of making the NHL, and making history, to which our family name will be forever attached. My mother, who'd been married to him for sixty-six years, was heartbroken. So when I returned to San Diego after the funeral, it comforted me to know that I still had brothers and sisters in Fredericton who would keep an eye on her.

My father's death and Chandra's birth in the same year were two life events that focused me on what I planned to do for my wife and daughter, and for myself, before my time on earth ran out. I'd just left hockey forever, but I'd still lie awake at night thinking of ways to get back into it. I didn't see how I could.

But then other people did, and I began a life in hockey all over again.

14.

BACK IN THE NHL

I kept working in security at the Del, which meant I was home while Chandra was growing up. Over the years I'd take her to her games with AYSO, the soccer league for kids, so I was able to watch as she became a very good soccer player. Seeing my daughter play and enjoy sports was a joy, but it also made me miss the game that had been so good to me. Then, in 1990, San Diego got a new hockey team.

The Gulls swooped back into town that year with a franchise in the International Hockey League. I saw my chance to get back in the game, not as a player, but by doing anything I could to connect with the sport. They were coached by Mike O'Connell, a former Boston Bruin, which could give me an edge, as Bruins stick together. After all, I was well-known in the community, and I figured I could help them out.

I didn't know a soul in their front office when I made my way there to offer my services. But they knew who I was and were very happy to see me, which made me feel great. It's always nice to be welcomed—and I was welcomed into the new edition of the team with open arms. They asked me to work in community relations and ticket sales, reasoning that my profile in San Diego would help get fans in seats. They were right, and for the next seven years, although I kept working at the Del, I was the Gulls' top salesman.

To promote the team, and the game itself, I'd go to community dinners and events and would speak at schools. People listened, too—I had the experience to back up what I was saying, and many of them had been fans of the Gulls, and of me, back when I used to play for them. This public exposure, and especially speaking to students, turned out to be good training for what was coming next. Of course, I didn't know what was coming next at the time. All I knew was that I needed more hockey, somehow.

I also knew that I needed to deal with my blind right eye. For years I'd ignored its throbbing pain, a pain that sometimes felt as if someone were poking my eye socket with a penknife. Now that I wasn't playing hockey anymore, I was paying more attention to that eye. So I finally went to an ophthalmologist to ask if anything could be done.

He told me that we had two options: he could inject a solution into my dead eye and rebalance the pressure points, or he could surgically remove the eye and get me a prosthetic one.

I chose the second option. So the surgeon cut out my eye and replaced it with a fake one that looks just like the real thing. I clean it as you would a contact lens, pop it back in my eye socket, and away I go. If I don't clean it and it gets grit or a hair on it, then it can be just as annoying as the pain had been. So I'm quite thorough about keeping the prosthetic eyeball I can't see out of as good as new.

With my eye pain gone, I'd pretty much resigned myself to working in security until I retired in a couple of years. Or changed my fortune through some kind of hockey miracle.

More than half a decade later, in 1996, I was still in security and hoping for a shot with a team—working with players, managing a club, anything really—but by then I was going on sixty-one. I figured my chances were slim at best, and best wasn't looking very good at all. Still, I've never given up on anything. So when I'd wake up in the morning I'd tell myself that today just might be the day when I could get back into the game I loved so much. You just never knew. And all you had to be was ready for the chance.

That day came when, out of the blue Southern California skies, I received a phone call from Bryant McBride, the newly appointed vice-president of the NHL's diversity program.

Bryant, a black man, was born in Chicago but raised in Sault Ste. Marie, Ontario. He has a pretty impressive résumé of firsts. He was the first African American elected class president at the United States Military Academy at West Point, where he served as a cadet from 1984 to 1986. In 1988 he graduated from Connecticut's Trinity College, where he had been the first African American to be elected class president and was voted an All-American defenseman for Trinity's championship hockey team. In 1990, McBride got his master's degree in public administration from the John F. Kennedy School of Government at Harvard University. This was not a guy to sit around and wait for permission.

Bryant had been in a meeting in New York with, among others, Lou Vairo of USA Hockey (the game's governing body in the United States) when my name came up. Lou, who'd coached the U.S. national men's team and had been an assistant coach with the New Jersey Devils, was appointed director of special projects for USA Hockey in 1992. He and Bryant were discussing how they could join forces and open up the game to a more diverse range of kids. Hockey was, at the time, still a pretty white sport.

When they got to talking about how Jackie Robinson had broken baseball's color barrier in 1947, Lou said, "Well, we have our own Jackie Robinson in hockey." The room went dead quiet and then someone said, "Who is it?"

Lou Vairo, a native of Brooklyn, had seen me play in the old Madison Square Garden with the Bruins, and even score a goal against his beloved Blueshirts. So he told the group about me. (It's one of the things that hockey could do better, and that I'm trying to do with my own work: to tell the game's own great story more widely and with more volume.)

Bryant McBride, a hockey guy of note himself, had never heard of me. He was amazed to learn that hockey had its own Jackie Robinson—and saw an opportunity. Bryant wondered if I might like to get involved with the NHL's diversity program. Did anyone know where I was? No one did.

This was 1996, so you couldn't just go and Google me because there was no Google. But Lou Vairo remembered that I'd been playing out in Southern California, and even remembered that I'd been a San Diego Gull. (That's how real hockey guys think. They remember players and their teams the way chefs remember recipes.) As it happened, Bryant knew a couple of FBI agents in San Diego, so he called them up and asked if they could help.

Now, I've never been in trouble with the law (well, except that time when a neighbor in Fredericton complained about our baseball games on the street and the police came). The most I've received by way of law enforcement (by which I mean those guys in zebra sweaters) has been time in the penalty box. In short, I was not known to the FBI.

But I *was* known to the security business, thanks to my guard card. So within a few hours the FBI guys called Bryant back and told him they'd found me.

That's when I got the phone call I'd been waiting for since 1961—a phone call from the NHL. But this was one I'd never even dreamed of.

Bryant McBride told me he was directing an NHL diversity program, a new venture to attract a more diverse group of young players to the game. He laid it all out for me (or rather, he laid out where he thought it might go, since he was creating it from the ground up), and then posed the question: Would I like to get in on the ground floor of this wonderful idea and see how high we could raise it?

I thought about it for as long as it takes to shoot a puck into an empty net. Yes, I said, I would like that very much.

Bryant wanted to choose twenty-four hockey-playing kids from different ethnic communities—black or Latino or Asian—from all over North America and give them a big-league treat. He would fly them to Boston to play in a special hockey tournament to be called "The Willie O'Ree All-Star Weekend." And, of course, he wanted me to be there, too.

You can't imagine how thrilling this was. That morning I'd woken up, had breakfast, kissed Deljeet and Chandra goodbye, and gone to work at the Del, just as I'd done for the last few years. Then that evening, with one phone call, my life changed. I was back in the NHL.

If you had told me that something like this would one day happen when I was playing for the Bruins, I would have said you were crazy. I thought I had reached the pinnacle then, but now Bryant McBride was offering me another pinnacle to reach. To change the complexion of the game I loved.

I told Bryant I'd have to get the time off at the Del to go to the All-Star Weekend named after me. My boss knew that l was trying to get back into hockey, so when I asked him for time off and explained why, he said, "Go and have fun."

And you'd have to be dead not to have had fun at that All-Star Weekend. The kids, from all across the continent, were uniformly great, and they sure could play hockey. They played one game at a local rink followed by one at the Fleet Center, where the Bruins played. They were in awe playing on an actual NHL rink. I certainly remembered the feeling of stepping onto NHL ice for the first time. Just being on it made you better.

It was also the NHL's All-Star Weekend, so I got to see many of the friends I'd made thirty-five years earlier, back when I played for the Bruins: Fernie Flaman, Bronco Horvath, Fleming Mackell, Leo Boivin, and Johnny Bucyk. We had a great time remembering the old days. Whenever I'd needed backup on account of knuckleheads giving me grief, all those guys—Bucyk, Stasiuk, Charlie Burns, Jerry Toppazzini—would ride to the rescue. Unless we were leading an odd-man rush, I was never left outnumbered. So seeing them again was like being back in the locker room when I'd first met them in 1958. But this time with a difference.

It was Johnny Bucyk who brought up my blind right eye. He couldn't imagine how I'd pulled it off. They knew I was fast and that I could check, but they'd had no idea I could only see out of one eye. How had I done it? This Hockey Hall of Famer was looking at me with a kind of awe, which in itself was heartening. I told him I'd just done what I always did, and played the game. Then I added how great it was to see them out of one eye again now, and that I hoped they'd help me with my new mission: to bring more kids into the game that had made us all so happy.

One Bruin who could not have been more generous with his time was that obscure defenseman named Bobby Orr. As one of the greatest Bruins to ever wear the black and gold, he had many demands on his time that weekend, but he always had time for the kids. He signed autographs all day long, until every kid—and every mother, grandmother, uncle, and cousin—had the great Number 4's signature. He was such an inspiration to the kids, and to me. Bobby Orr is a gentleman. It has been a privilege to get to know him and to have his help.

The weekend went by far too fast and I was sorry to leave, but I had a feeling I could make the next All-Star Weekend just as good.

Now that we'd pulled off our first success, though, Bryant McBride had other plans. He asked me to go to Bellingham, Washington, to help psychologist Dr. Bob Osterman with a sports dinner he was hosting. Bob was running an innovative program, called Creative Concepts, that was using hockey to help kids who were having problems with the law. The idea was that, in playing the game, they'd be taught how to better control their anger. Now, that may seem kind of counterintuitive, given what a fast and passionate game hockey is, one frequently punctuated by the very anger he was trying to manage. But I knew from my playing days just how much discipline and control you needed in order to play the game well.

Bob knew it, too, but he was worried no one would show up at his dinner. So, to help promote the event, I went on the radio in Bellingham and even visited a juvenile detention center to speak to kids about the program. In the end, they had to put in more tables to seat all the people who came. I was now seeing the power I had to change lives for the better through the very game that had made my life so rich.

The following year, the NHL asked me to attend the next Willie O'Ree All-Star Weekend, this time in San Jose. Once again I had to ask for time off from the Del, and again my boss had to find someone to replace me. Actually, I worried I might lose my job, still not quite seeing that maybe this NHL gig would be more long-term than I'd imagined.

Then the next year, 1998, I was invited to the NHL All-Star Game in Vancouver, which coincided with the fortieth anniversary of my breaking the color barrier. This time, though, the NHL wanted me to help break another barrier. Bryant said, "Willie, I've been talking to Gary Bettman about you and what you've been doing, and we were wondering . . . what would it take for you to join the NHL Diversity Task Force on a permanent basis?"

Hearing that the NHL commissioner himself was rooting for me made me a believer. Just as I'd been invited into the Bruins all those years ago, the big time was calling me once more. I thought about it for about one second and said, "Two weeks' notice."

Meaning the notice I'd need to give the Del. Then I'd be free and clear to join the NHL. After spending years as a player trying to get into the league—and then back into it— here I was, getting another chance. At age sixty-three.

I had to laugh: I wouldn't have believed this if I'd read it in a book. I, the first black man to play in the NHL, was going to help minority kids find a dream and then live it. I'd be helping them skate on the same ice I'd skated on. I was going to be a pioneer once again.

15.

A CLEAN SHEET OF ICE

Here's the funny thing about life. You don't know the meaning of what you've done until you've done it. You can't. All you can expect of yourself is to keep doing your best. All you can do is what you know is right. Even when it's hard. Even when the odds don't look good. Even when the easier path is laid out in front of you. Do that, and things may just work out.

That's not the same thing as saying you're always going to win. No one wins every time. You may lose more than your fair share. There are no guarantees.

Well, just one. If you *don't* stick to your guns, you're definitely not going to win. So give yourself that shot. You're the only one who can.

Did I set out to be the name of the NHL's diversity program when I stepped onto the outdoor rink in Fredericton during the Second World War? I did not. Did I think about helping inner-city kids in the United States when I was racking up goals in the Quebec league? Not at all. What I was thinking about, though, was doing my best. And I'm grateful every day that I did.

Joining the NHL to help guide its diversity program from pretty much the beginning was the type of challenge I love: to do something new and bold with an outcome that could only be called a win for everyone. My favorite kind of victory.

At that point there were about four or five programs; we have thirty-four now. My duties then and now are to travel around to the different programs and help these kids, on and off the ice, develop their hockey skills and life skills.

Our slogan, "Hockey Is for Everyone," is exactly what that means—we won't turn any boy or girl away. And over the past twenty-three years I've seen a big increase in the number of kids who want to play the game, and who've realized, because of us, that they can.

One of those players is Gerald Coleman, who was with our program called PUCK, Positive Uplifting of Chicago Kids. I met Gerald when he was thirteen, just a skinny little black kid who wanted to be a goaltender. Everyone tried to talk him out of it by pointing out that he was black, as if that fact alone would put the brakes on his dream. It staggers me still that we can think that way, but luckily for hockey, Gerald didn't. In him I saw my young self when he said he was going to make the NHL and that no one was going to stop him. People tried, for sure. When he was a high school freshman, a gym teacher kept the tired old blockade going by asking Gerald why he was "playing a white man's game." Well, because he liked it. And because in our program he'd seen kids of every color playing hockey.

Since we started the program we've had nearly fifty thousand kids participate. Gerald Coleman was the first to make it to the NHL—when, in 2003, he was selected 224th overall by the Tampa Bay Lightning. Gerald had come off a terrific junior career with the Ontario Hockey League's London Knights, having won the Dave Pinkney Trophy twice as part of the goaltending team with the lowest goals-against average. And the season after Gerald was drafted by the Lightning, he would win the Memorial Cup.

He wound up playing two games for Tampa, then spent the rest of his career in the minor pro league before injuries made him hang up his skates in 2014. But I'm very proud of Gerald and what he accomplished. I saw a lot of myself in him.

I also see a lot of myself in kids who come off the ice crying because someone has said something awful to them. I do everything I can to change how they hear those insults. I tell them that they're just words, and that the best way to deal with the people who think they can hurt you with those words is to be your best and to show them your game on the ice.

I know: sometimes I didn't always take my own advice. But once a young player learns to believe that the power is with them, not with the racist, they're transformed.

One such case hit me close to home, since it happened to a young player in Fredericton. Taylor Leblanc, who is of Acadian, Jamaican, and Chinese descent, is the eldest of three hockey-playing brothers. He was twelve—the same age I was—when someone made a racial remark that left him puzzled and hurt. He'd never heard it before and wasn't sure how to respond.

When a mutual friend in Fredericton told me about it, I gave Taylor a call. I know what it's like for these kids. But I also think it's tougher for them today than it was for me because we live in a society where it's become acceptable to publicly disparage your fellow human beings for whatever reason—their skin color, their place of origin, their gender or sexual orientation. Maybe it's always been like that. But now, with so many ways to broadcast hateful views, it seems much louder. And there's already just so much pressure on you as a kid.

So I called Taylor up and we talked about it. I told him the best way to respond was with his play, and by ignoring the bullies and the bigots, because ignoring them was the thing that drove them crazy.

The racism never stops, but it's how you deal with it that makes the difference. I sometimes wish these ignorant, mean-spirited people could see the effort these kids need to make and the circumstances they need to overcome just to get on the ice. Not everyone has a pond to play on or parents who can make a rink in the backyard. Hockey is expensive, no doubt about it. And it's become a lot more so since I started playing eighty years ago. You need to wear all the protective gear, which costs about $700, and which a lot of families can't afford. So if these kids want to play hockey and don't have the money, we'll pick up the tab. And if they don't like it, then someone else will get the gear and no hard feelings. We're only trying to help kids who want to play, and no kid who wants to play is ever turned away.

I've learned a lot in my role as ambassador for the NHL and its diversity outreach. But one lesson I wish I hadn't learned is seeing how this rich, privileged continent of ours still has so many problems to fix when it comes to how we treat kids, how we treat our future.

I've been in too many schools where teachers have to buy the textbooks, pens, and paper for the students. I was in a school in Harlem that had concrete floors covered with ceramic tiles—whenever you'd move a chair it screeched across the floor in a way that would make fingernails on a blackboard sound pleasant. The problem was solved when the principal, out of her own pocket, bought tennis balls for each chair leg in that school. In fact, while I was talking to the kids at her school, I noticed that she'd pop out of class a couple of times, on the hour. Later she told me she had to move her car or she'd get a ticket. There was no parking space for the principal of this school.

One funny thing happened there, though. At the end of my talk, I gave the students signed hockey cards with a photo of me as a Boston Bruin—young, proud, and looking great in my Bruins jersey. Then, when I asked the kids if there were any questions, one little girl put up her hand.

"Who is that in the photo?"

Everyone laughed, and I assured her that it was me.

She wasn't buying it. "It doesn't look like you," she said, and everyone laughed again.

So I told her to do a little time travel as I mimed the pose in the photograph, and to imagine me as a guy not much older than she was. And then I saw her smile in delight. She got it. I was who I said I was.

One time in Pennsylvania, I had more kids coming to hear me than I had cards to give out. I never like to see a kid go away empty-handed, so I told the students that if they didn't get a card I'd sign anything they wanted me to sign.

This didn't make the school administration happy, since it added about another hour to my event as kids brought up backpacks, lunch kits, and yes, textbooks for me to sign. I signed them all, including the back of a kid's jacket. I could imagine the conversation he'd have about that later with his mother.

When I first started with the diversity program I'd sometimes be on the road for three weeks out of the month, but today my schedule is gentler. During the course of the year I'm away for about one week every month, from the beginning of the season in October till the end of it in June. It's still a lot like being a player. I travel, I go to the rink, I work out, I have my afternoon nap—a player staple on game days—and I get to meet wonderful people across the continent.

The Adeniye family certainly counts as among the best. I first met Ayodele "Ayo" Adeniye in 2005, when he was just six years old. His mother, Lisa Ramos, would drive me around Columbus whenever I was in town for one of my clinics, and Ayo—who was enrolled in the Columbus Ice Hockey Club, part of the NHL's "Hockey Is for Everyone" program—was always asking me questions, getting my take on what it took to play in the NHL.

He'd gotten interested in hockey at about the same age I did—when he was three. He was at a friend's birthday party at a local ice rink when he saw a high school hockey game on an adjacent rink—and told his mother that this was the game he wanted to play. Now, his mother comes from an athletic family: her grandfather played baseball in the Negro Leagues and her father had not only won the state championship in high jump and cross country but had played basketball for the army in Europe as well. But, like so many families of color, hockey wasn't part of their sporting history.

And yet Ayo persisted. When Lisa enrolled him in basketball as a little kid, instead of running around like the rest of the children, he moved about the court in ice-skating motions. It must have been pretty funny to see, but Ayo was serious: he wanted to play hockey. His mother got the message.

It was more than just being black hockey players that made us bond. Ayo had eye problems, too. He was born with misaligned eyes, which led to a few surgeries to rebalance his eye muscles and literally get his eyes straightened out. Every time I was in Columbus we'd get together. I watched him grow both as a person and as a hockey player.

But it wasn't all a smooth ride for him, either—especially when he got cut from the Ohio Blue Jackets' AAA hockey program. He could have quit then. But he remembered what I'd told him: "If you think you can, you can." So he joined the Cleveland Junior Lumberjacks, his mother driving him to and from the city, a two-hour trip each way. Ayo played hard, and eventually worked his way back onto the Columbus team.

Today that little six-year-old is a six-foot-five, two-hundred-pound defenseman who, beginning in the 2020 season, will be playing for the University of Alabama-Huntsville Chargers, an NCAA Division I team in the Western Collegiate Hockey Association. And I bet we see him in the NHL before too long, patrolling the blue line for a team smart enough to give him a shot.

I was in Columbus in February 2018 when the Blue Jackets held their "Hockey Is for Everyone Night." During pre-game warm-ups, Blue Jackets defenseman and "Hockey Is For Everyone" ambassador Seth Jones and the team used rainbow-colored Pride tape on their sticks and practiced with Pride-themed pucks. The program wants to include everyone—and on this night we were celebrating LGBTQ athletes, coaches, and fans.

Over the past two decades we've brought the same message to thousands of kids—from urban to rural and in between, from kids of color to the LGBTQ community to people with physical challenges who play sled hockey: that hockey is indeed for everyone.

And that there are more places than ever to play the game. When I first started playing I was on the ice every day: after all, I lived in a cold place with natural ice for nearly half the year. During the winter I could skate anytime I wanted. But today I'm happy to note that there are rinks everywhere, regardless of climate—Harlem in New York, Texas, Georgia, Carolina, Miami, Chicago, Los Angeles, Arizona, all over the place. And it doesn't always have to be ice. In-line rinks are big here in San Diego, and there's even one named after me in Boston. It doesn't matter to me whether kids are playing on ice or pavement. They just need to be able to play.

I love many things about my job, but what I love most is seeing the excitement kids have about playing the game. Just as I did, they love feeling as if they're flying when they skate, the breeze whipping past them as they go. They feel as if they can do anything. And as I tell them, "If you think you can, you can, and if you think you can't, you're probably right."

Kids who've never been out of their own inner-city neighborhoods are amazed that playing hockey gets them a ride on an airplane and a place at my All-Star Weekend. Kids who've never been given anything get free hockey equipment donated by the NHL and USA Hockey. Kids who've been in trouble at school or with the law find a place where they can be taught teamwork. And as any hockey player knows, if you don't have teamwork, you don't have a team.

When kids ask me what it was like when people called me names, I tell them, "I just looked at myself as a man, and knew that people had to accept me as a hockey player because of my skills and ability."

There's a saying I like a lot: "Each man is three men: who he thinks he is, who others think he is, and who he really is." I tell the kids to know who they really are and be true to themselves. Everything will flow smoothly after that. If I can just get that message through to one person, then I'm happy.

When I go to the rink to give the kids some on-ice help, or when I talk to them in the locker room or in their school auditorium, I see the pride in their eyes. I see that my words, and my story, connect with them in a way that will help them love this great game the way I love it. They don't need to win the Stanley Cup, although every hockey player has won it in their mind's eye a couple of times, to be sure. They just have to know they can play if they want to play, and take it all from there.

16.

THE CALL, PART 2

After my hockey career ended, whenever the Hockey Hall of Fame would come up in conversation people were surprised to learn I wasn't in it. "But you broke the color barrier!" they'd say. And I would agree, but gently remind them that Baseball Hall-of-Famer Jackie Robinson had also won Rookie of the Year and I had not. There were certainly similarities between us, but they weren't going to elect me to the Hall of Fame out of charity. I did wonder, though, if one day I could maybe get there by some other means.

I've been recognized by many organizations, and I'm grateful for their acknowledgment of my life in hockey. I was elected to the New Brunswick Sports Hall of Fame in 1984, a wonderful distinction, and one my mother was alive to see. She died three years later at the great age of ninety-three. So

I was happy that both my parents got to see what I'd achieved and the honor I'd brought to the O'Ree family name.

In 1992 my hometown of Fredericton put me up on its Sports Wall of Fame. Then, in 2003, the NHL awarded me the Lester Patrick Trophy for my contributions to hockey in the United States. I'd played for Lester Patrick's son Lynn in Boston, so that was especially sweet. It felt as if I were connecting to the team and to that epic time in my life all over again.

In 2005 I was named to the Order of New Brunswick, and the following year I was honored with my induction into the Black Ice Hockey and Sports Hall of Fame in Nova Scotia.

The fiftieth anniversary year of my NHL debut was a big one for me as well. In 2008 the league honored me at their All-Star Game in Atlanta, which has had a significant role in the story of civil rights in the United States. The theme that year was diversity, so not only was my achievement celebrated but also that of John Paris Jr., who in 1994 became the first man of African heritage to coach a pro hockey team when he became bench boss of the International Hockey League's Atlanta Knights.

I also got to drop the ceremonial puck for Jarome Iginla, who was on the Western Conference All-Star team and whose father hails from Nigeria. Iginla was not only an excellent hockey player but a pretty fine baseball player as well, winning the job of catcher for the Canadian national junior team. He's a great guy, and serves with me as an NHL diversity ambassador. He's even said that I had inspired his path to pro hockey.

In 2008 I was inducted into the San Diego Hall of Champions, and in the same year I received an award from San Diego State University for Outstanding Commitment to Diversity and Cross-Cultural Understanding.

The biggest honor to me that year, maybe in my personal top two, was having a new sports complex named after me in Fredericton. As a kid playing on the city's ponds I could never have dreamed of Willie O'Ree Place—an amazing recreation facility on the north side of the Saint John River, a little more than two miles away from the street where I grew up. It's big and it's welcoming, with a large glass front to let you see inside and want to come in. And what you'll find is not one but two NHL-sized ice surfaces, eleven spacious dressing rooms, offices for officials and event organizers, and an indoor walking track where you can look down at the shiny rink below. I've very proud of the fact that it houses a gallery of photos depicting Fredericton's celebration of sport along with three rooms for community use, food and drink services, a wellness center, a seasonal youth center, and an indoor skateboard park. It's fully accessible, too, so you can walk in or wheel in and see its wonders. It gives me chills to think that generations of people will be able to enjoy this center and maybe learn a bit about me as they do. And carry it all forward.

In 2010 I was astonished to be inducted into the Order of Canada by Governor General Michaëlle Jean. This is the highest civilian honor a Canadian citizen can receive, and in joining people like Maurice "The Rocket" Richard and Jean Béliveau, you could say that I did make their team in the end.

—

Back on January 18, 1958, when I pulled on that black and gold Bruins jersey for the first time, I never ever imagined that such recognition would come to me. So on January 17, 2018, when the Boston Bruins honored me on the eve of the sixtieth anniversary of that historic moment with a pre-game celebration, it nearly brought me to tears.

They even ran a segment of that game as it had appeared on television. There I was, up on the big screen in TD Garden, playing my first game all over again. I'd been so proud to be there, so full of dreams. The day had already been wonderful, with Boston mayor Marty Walsh and NHL commissioner Gary Bettman announcing that one of the city's street hockey rinks would be named after me, along with the league that went with it. The mayor added that he was making January 18, 2018, "Willie O'Ree Day" in Boston. Back when I was riding the train in from Roxbury to suit up for the Bruins, if you'd told me that would happen I'd have thought someone had cracked you over the head with a hockey stick.

And just as they had sixty years before, the Bruins were playing the Montreal Canadiens that night. I received a standing ovation when I walked out in my Bruins jersey, number 22 of course, along with four kids from Boston's SCORE, a program that brings the great game to inner city kids. Those kids stood proudly beside me as I dropped the ceremonial puck for Bruins captain Zdeno Chara and

Montreal's Max Pacioretty. After that it looked like Montreal might ruin my party when they scored thirty-one seconds into the game on a deflection, but then the Bruins came roaring back to defeat the Canadiens 4–1, putting the icing on the anniversary cake of that glorious night.

As I said when I began this tale, my story has many beginnings—and that night in Boston ushered in another one. And it all connected back to my hometown. For it started the next morning when a fine New Brunswick sportswriter named Bill Hunt fired up his computer and wrote his weekly sports column for Fredericton's *The Daily Gleaner*. And it was a much different story than the last time a New Brunswick sports journalist had written about me, when I was ambushed with news of being traded from Boston.

He was planning to list the things I had accomplished as a kind of round-up piece about me, but as he wrote, one big question nagged at him: How was it that the player who'd broken into the NHL in the Jim Crow United States—six years before the Civil Rights Act became law and a year before the Red Sox fielded their first black player—wasn't in the Hockey Hall of Fame? The title of his column answered the question: "Time to Put Willie in the Hall of Fame."

The next day Hunt wrote a follow-up piece that explained the nuts and bolts of the nomination process and how anyone could put together a package for it. Of course, the trick is getting that nomination package past the selection committee with 75 percent of the votes, since getting elected is no easy thing. But when my Fredericton friends David and Brenda Sansom read Bill Hunt's piece, they got to work.

David Sansom has known my family since he was eleven years old, which was a while ago. (He'd been out fishing on the Saint John River when we all pulled up for a family picnic and invited him to join us.) Today David is among my group of friends who go back decades; his wife, Brenda, is a more recent member, but we're teammates nonetheless. It was Brenda's experience as former Fredericton city councillor that galvanized into action what would eventually be called Team Willie.

At first, things didn't move too fast. So Brenda, David, and Bill had to beat the drums loudly, going on local radio shows, meeting people at community centers, spreading the word and putting out the call for letters of support. Now, we live in a world where everyone seems to be writing things all the time—on Twitter, Instagram, email—but it takes a lot to write a letter, especially if you're not a writer and especially if you're feeling the pressure about what that letter is supposed to accomplish.

The first ones came into Brenda and David from my fishing pals, my card-playing buddies, and people who knew me around Fredericton and the Maritimes more broadly.

And then, with about two weeks to go before the nomination package was due, "no later than midnight April 15," letters started flooding in. I don't think Brenda and David were getting too much sleep as they and Bill Hunt struggled to keep up with them all. Team Willie told me they received dozens of letters of support—from everyday people and hockey fans, from current and former NHLers, from past premiers of New Brunswick, from a sitting premier, from a former lieutenant governor, from a Canadian senator, and from a number of community groups.

Some of the letters that moved me most came from black NHL players. Joel Ward, at the time a forward with the San Jose Sharks, wrote a two-page letter that explained how my life in hockey had influenced his own. "What Willie has done for the game cannot be put into words. But it can be recognized," Ward said. "When you think about 'builders' of the game of hockey, who has sacrificed more and given more of himself to the game of hockey than Willie O'Ree?"

Another black player, Wayne Simmonds, who at the time played for the Philadelphia Flyers, wrote a piece supporting me in *The Players Tribune*, an online journal where athletes tell their stories. I'd met Wayne during his rookie season with the L.A. Kings and thought he had a great future ahead of him. He had the on-ice talent and the off-ice personality that can't be taught. In his piece he said that, in meeting me,

> *I was meeting my hero. For every single kid who was ever told to "stick to basketball," Willie was like the first man on the moon. He wasn't just a hockey player. He was an astronaut. Without Willie, there would be no Jarome Iginla. There would be no Grant Fuhr, or P.K. Subban or Ray Emery or Dustin Byfuglien, or so many others who have had the honor of playing in this great league. There would definitely be no Wayne Simmonds.*

Team Willie also got a letter of support from P.K. Subban's father, Karl, one that meant the world to me. P.K. is another fine athlete and person; he now plays for the New Jersey Devils while one brother, Malcolm, plays goal for the Las Vegas Golden Knights and his other brother, Jordan, a defenseman like P.K., plays pro in Austria. Karl Subban used to take little P.K. skating at Toronto's Nathan Phillips Square late at night—Karl was holding down two jobs, and that was the only time he had. His words about me affected me as much as I'd affected him.

Willie stepped on the ice with the Boston Bruins in 1958, the year when I was born, and made hockey history. He is a pioneer and a trailblazer. Willie achieved in the face of adversity. He changed the game and he changed society and he changed minds. Willie O'Ree's story must not be forgotten. He has made it possible for my boys to have the NHL dream and to believe they could achieve it. He changed hockey which is now for everyone. Hockey needed him and so does the Hockey Hall of Fame. The time is right!

And so, with support like that, Brenda, David, and Bill managed to get my seventy-page nomination package into the Hockey Hall of Fame just before the deadline. After that came a couple of months of waiting while the selection committee did its work.

———

As it happened, a film crew was following me at the same time; they were making a film, called *Willie*, about my life. So on the day the Hall of Fame was set to make its announcement of the 2018 Honoured Members, I was at home in La Mesa, where I've lived for thirty years, with my wife Deljeet and our future son-in-law Talib—along with Bryant McBride, who was one of the film's producers, and Montreal-born Laurence Mathieu-Léger, who was its director. We were all waiting for the phone call while the camera rolled.

Meanwhile Laurence had another camera unit at David and Brenda's Fredericton home. They were having a party— optimists that they are—and the plan was for me to call them as soon as I heard from the Hall of Fame, which was supposed to happen between nine a.m. and noon my time.

I have to admit that I was nervous that morning, just as I'd been for my first game in the NHL. Now that the pinnacle of hockey life was within reach, I wanted to touch it so badly that I didn't know what I would do if I failed.

There's a wonderful scene in the film where it's getting close to noon, everyone's nerves are getting frayed, and Bryant McBride comes into my trophy room to show me the time on his phone: 11:11. I'm not superstitious, but 11:11 is a time to make a wish, which is what Bryant told me to do.

I did, and right then, the phone rang.

We had four different phones out on the kitchen counter, and at first I wasn't sure which one was ringing. But I managed to pick up the right one—because on the other end of the line was John Davidson, chair of the Hall of Fame selection committee, along with Lanny McDonald, a former chair and a great NHL player.

They told me I'd been elected to the Hockey Hall of Fame as a builder—a person who's helped "build" the game forward. I was truly at a loss for words, which you'll see if you watch the film. I was overwhelmed with happiness and pride, and, because I'm so competitive, a little relief. I'd wanted to win this one so badly, and now I had.

Talib had two phones up, one filming it and one with Chandra on FaceTime so that she could see what was happening in our kitchen, which was just one big celebration. And there was another one waiting to break out.

Back in Fredericton, Brenda and David and my friends— some of whom had gathered in the Cabin restaurant, my favorite restaurant in the world and one of Canada's top seven road-trip food stops—were waiting for my call to tell them the news, good or bad. And since the news was so good, I decided to have a little fun with them. I tapped in their number, and when Brenda answered I told her I'd gotten a call from the Hall of Fame. Then I paused dramatically. Finally she asked nervously, "How did it go?" "Pretty good," I said, and paused again. Then I let it all come out.

Brenda shrieked with joy and with a few tears, too. She and David and Bill Hunt and Bryant McBride and a cast of hundreds who'd supported me on this latest journey had made it all happen.

———

In November 2018 Deljeet and I made the trip to Toronto for my induction. With us were Brenda and David, my pal Junior Doherty and his wife, Lynn, and a pretty impressive group of my hockey comrades: goalie Martin Brodeur, right-winger Martin St. Louis, Team Canada star Jayna Hefford, Russian legend Alexander Yakushev, and NHL commissioner Gary Bettman.

The Hall of Fame was established in 1943, with players and builders first inducted into its ranks two years later, in 1945. Since 1992 it's been housed in the beautiful old Bank of Montreal building in Toronto, where each November they host the induction ceremony.

In fact, my 1958 accomplishment—certainly part of the great story they tell of hockey's history—had already gained me a presence in the Hall. Beside a life-sized portrait of a young me, leaning on my stick in my Bruins uniform, is some text explaining what happened on that evening of January 18. The Hall also contains a glass display case celebrating diversity, and in it stands one of my scuffed Northwood hockey sticks, its nearly straight blade with black tape around it and my surname written on the handle. Now, though, I was about to become an Honoured Member, my name and story on a plaque in hockey's pantheon.

The entire Hall of Fame weekend was such a marvelous experience. All the inductees were given private receptions with our families, as well as a meet-and-greet with the media and fans. The feeling was one of celebration from beginning to end, and it made me think of the long journey I'd made to get to this place.

And since each new Honoured Member is expected to make a speech, I'd had to prepare mine. I was given five minutes, which I think is about the right amount of time to talk to any group without letting them talk back, but my speech was clocking in at eight minutes. So I asked the NHL for help, and Mike Sullivan in the New York office rode to the rescue. We worked on the speech together, timing it with a stopwatch, until finally, with Mike's surgical wisdom, I had it down to five minutes and sixteen seconds and was ready to deliver it to the people gathered in the Hall of Fame's auditorium on Monday, November 12, 2018.

I was sitting with Deljeet, Chandra and Talib, Gary Bettman and his wife, and Bryant McBride, the man who'd brought me back to the NHL. By that time I'd gone over my speech and rehearsed it a dozen times—I wanted to make sure I delivered it well for all the people who'd helped me make it into the Hall of Fame.

Even so, I was nervous. Much more nervous than I thought I would be, but when the great Edmonton Oilers goalie— and fellow black hockey player—Grant Fuhr summoned me to the stage and handed me the plaque honoring my election, my nerves passed and I was once again on the ice, doing what I do. And this is what I said:

> *At the age of fourteen I had set two goals for myself. To play professional hockey and to one day play in the NHL. All I wanted was to be a hockey player. All I needed was an opportunity.*

*To be here with you tonight is simply overwhelming.
There are no words to express how humble and grateful
I am to be part of the Hockey Hall of Fame.*

*I thank the Selection Committee for the incredible honor
and offer heartfelt congratulations to my fellow inductees.*

*To my wife Deljeet, my daughter Chandra, I am thank-
ful to share this special moment with you.*

*Believe it or not, on January the 18, 1958, when I
stepped on the ice with the Bruins, it did not dawn on me
that I was breaking the color barrier. That's how focused I
was on making my dream come true.*

*I did not realize I had made history until I read it in the
paper the next day.*

*I have spent sixty-seven years of my life in hockey. Now,
as the NHL's ambassador, I travel across North America
introducing boys and girls to the game I love. We also focus
on life lessons hockey teaches us, and most importantly,
setting goals.*

*My mission is to give them the opportunity like the one
I was given.*

*Years ago I was doing an event in Los Angeles. Snoop
Dogg was there. We know he loves the game. But when I
got him out there on skates, he said, "Willie, I hope I don't
fall." I told him what I tell the kids. "If you fall, just get
back up."*

*As a teen, I looked up to Herbie and Ossie Carnegie
and Manny McIntyre. They paved the way for me; they
just never got the opportunity I did.*

When I lost the sight in my right eye playing junior, the doctor told me I would never play again. I refused to accept that. His words did not discourage me. They fueled me to try harder, to never give up.

Three years later, I broke the color barrier.

In life and sports, there are people who assist you along the way. My brother Richard was one of those people for me. When playing hockey together, he used to check me so hard that tears would come to my eyes. He wanted me to be ready for the pros.

My sister Betty encouraged me, too. She was there only when I told her about losing sight in my right eye. She believed in me and kept it a secret.

I would like to thank Lou Vairo from USA Hockey for recommending me to the NHL in 1996. I am grateful to Bryant McBride, who was the vice-president of the NHL's diversity program at that time. Many thanks to Ken Martin Jr. for your support and courage. Thank you Eustace King, my agent and friend. I would also like to thank the people of my hometown Fredericton, especially David and Brenda Sansom for spearheading my induction submission.

A heartfelt thanks to all the players and coaches I had the pleasure of playing with.

Finally, I would like to thank Commissioner Gary Bettman for trusting me with his vision for the future of the NHL, that hockey is for everyone.

We've made some substantial progress over the past twenty years. Lives are being changed thanks to your leadership, and your continued support allows us to make the game more diverse and inclusive each day. Thank you from the bottom of my heart for the opportunity you have given me, and congratulations, Gary, on your well-deserved induction tonight. I am honored to share this with you.

True strength comes from diversity and inclusion. It makes kids better, families better, it makes the game better. We know that because of players like Mike Marson, Jarome Iginla, Grant Fuhr, and so many others who have also broken barriers.

Tonight I am here to tell you we are not done because the work is not done. We have barriers to break and knock down, opportunities to give.

I leave this with you: When you return to your communities, take a look around, find a young boy or girl who needs the opportunity to play hockey, and give it to them.

You never know, they may make us dream.

Almost a year later I went back home to Fredericton for the premier screening in my hometown of the documentary film about me. I got to see all my old friends again—like Gus Mazzuca and Louis George and Junior Doherty and David and Brenda Sansom—along with so many other friends at the Cabin restaurant. I also got to talk to the media and tell my story all over again.

I was even invited back to my old high school, Fredericton High, to talk to the students. When I looked out on the crowded auditorium, I was astonished and delighted to see the diversity of the faces in that school. It seemed as if the whole world was there.

And the Fredericton High students gave me a gift: a black and gold jersey, same as the Boston Bruins, with my name and number 22 on the back. But this was no Bruins jersey, it was a Fredericton High jersey. More than seventy years after I'd been kicked off the school hockey team for breaking the collarbone of the coach's son, these students had put me back on the team. They even formed an honor guard, standing in two rows and tapping hockey sticks on the floor to celebrate me as I walked between them and on out of the room to my next rendezvous with hockey, and with my fellow humans.

So that, so far, is my story. But as I tell it, I see that it's not just about me. Not really. The name O'Ree appears in so many places, *on* so many places. But as much as I've been honored, it's not *my* name that appears in halls of fame or on public buildings. You can't own a name. It was there before me, and it will be here after I'm gone.

I've just tried to treat it with respect, by living up to the standard set by my ancestor. For as much as this is my story, it also belongs to Paris O'Ree. He achieved freedom for the sake of future generations. And he was vindicated by history, which has been made in his name. He was a pioneer whose legacy was further pioneering in his name. By taking up the challenge history issued him, he changed the future. So much would have been different without him. And in that sense, he is the author of this story.

But in the end, it's not about names, is it? It's not about taking credit. That's something else I can learn from Paris O'Ree. He's not asking for credit. Credit is beside the point. What his story shows, it seems to me, is that history lays a challenge out before each one of us. We all have the opportunity to do the right thing for the generations that follow. Even when it's hard. Even when there's reason to doubt that it will all work out. There is always risk. But when future generations are at stake, the greater risk is doing nothing.

I'd like to think I may have inspired others. That would be a fine accomplishment. I would be proud of that. But when I think of Paris O'Ree and what he went through, I'm reminded that whatever I've been able to do was possible only because of what he had the courage to do. If he'd done nothing, I could have done nothing. But courage begets courage. Good begets good. When courage and goodness wither within us, they wither in the future. When we nurture them, we nurture the future. We nurture generations to come.

I was given freedom, and because of that, I can help offer it to others. And while I offer it to others I gain more of it for myself. Because generosity frees us. Courage frees us. Much has been given to us. It falls to us to pass it on.

And I will.

ACKNOWLEDGMENTS

I have been lucky to receive help along my journey from many people, and it would take another book to thank them all. So, I would like to thank the people who made much of the story I tell within these pages possible, beginning with my mother Rosebud, and father Harry, who gave me all the love and support a guy could ever want. They made it possible for me to pursue my dream. I am grateful to all my twelve brothers and sisters, but especially to my brother Richard, who taught me how to play the game of hockey, and much about how to live my life, and to my sister Betty, who kept my secret because she believed in my dream as much as I did. In the hockey world, there are many to thank, but I am especially grateful to Stan Maxwell, my teammate for so many years; to Punch Imlach, who brought me up to give me a shot at the NHL, and to Milt Schmidt, who gave it to me. My Boston Bruins teammate, the great Johnny Bucyk, was always encouraging, and really, I thank all the wonderful teammates I had on every team, along with NHL Commissioner Gary Bettman, and the NHL family.

I have been blessed by my friends, and have managed to keep friendships from childhood until now. I am grateful to my manager Eustace King, the vision of Nick Garrison of Penguin Random House, the tireless work of Roger Freet of Folio Literary Management and my friend and writing teammate Michael McKinley for helping me to tell the tale within these pages.

Thank you to my family.

Last but most I thank my wife and partner of 51 years, Deljeet Manak. Thank you for your patience and encouragement.

INDEX